GLUTTONY
MORE IS MORE

SIN SERIES

VOLUME I

Gluttony

MORE IS MORE

NAN LYONS

RED ROCK PRESS, NEW YORK

Copyright © 1999, by Red Rock Press
ISBN: 0-9669573-0-X
Published by Red Rock Press
New York, New York
U.S.A.
www.redrockpress.com

Cover art: Colored, large detail of a Gustave Doré (1832-1883) woodcut of "Gargantua," for a privately printed volume, *The Works of Rabelais.*

Back cover art: *Les Noces Alsaciennes* by Paul Kaufmann From *Les Fastes de Bacchus et Comus* by G. Oberle, New York Academy of Medicine Library.

Grateful acknowledgment is made to Sylvia Carter, E. Clarke Reilly and Bernadette Wheeler for creating, compiling, translating, adapting, and testing the "Carte Blanche" recipes expressly for *Gluttony: More is More.*

PRINTED IN HONG KONG

TABLE OF CONTENTS

CARTE BLANCHE RECIPES

Edited by Sylvia Carter & E. Clarke Reilly

:THIS LITTLE PIG:
WENT TO MARKET

CHAPTER ONE

SEPARATION

OF CHURCH AND FATE

Here we stand, on the threshold of a whole new century in which the joys of excess may prove to be even more unrestrained, not to mention more creative, than ever before. The new millennium brings with it the heady possibility of leaving the sins of the past thousand years behind and trading up to a whole new standard of deliciously sinful behavior. If we are to be thrust into a new age filled with even more insatiable appetites and greater self-indulgence, now might be the perfect time to examine more closely the most comforting of the Seven Deadly Sins, gluttony.

"Let us eat and drink for tomorrow we shall die."
—ISAIAH 22:13

FORBIDDEN FRUIT SALAD

Long after the *Old Testament* was written, theologians may have labeled Eve's desire for that infamous apple of her eye Original Sin, but any card-carrying food fanatic will recognize at once what her problem was. Temptation, in Eve's case, was that most succulent of apples, touted by that cheeky serpent as simply irresistible.

Esau was even more emotional when it came to dealing with his food fantasies. He was so driven by his hunger that he bartered away his birthright for a bowl of pottage. Or maybe he was just in the mood for a mess of lentils.

The interpretation of sin in the old days was definitely in the eyes of the beholder. If the beholder happened to be the Church, then sin was characterized as anything that took one away from the dedicated worship of God.

In the 600s, the *Koran*, the sacred book of Islam, offered: "Children of Adam, put your minds and bodies in a state of tidiness at every time and place of worship, and eat and drink but be not immoderate." (7:32)

All in all, gluttony, or gorging oneself into a sublime state of bliss, was a spiritual breach of the contract to worship God above all else. Put that in your Peking Duck and smoke it.

Summer, 1563, by Giusseppe Arcimboldo

Vexational

I'm vexed as a stinging nettle
By cowards waving flags with mettle;
By hunting hawks in sorry fettle,
By skimpy meat in a mammoth kettle.
I hate by good St. Martin's sign,
A pint of water drowning in my wine!
—Monk of Montaudon, circa 1200

Deprive and Conquer

In the 1200s, Thomas Aquinas, in his most famous theological work, *Summa Theologica*, expanded and refined the ground rules for understanding the meaning of Christian doctrine. Heading the list of ways errant members of the Church found to exclude God from their lives was a short and, by today's standards, seemingly harmless clutch of transgressions, which became known as the Seven Deadly Sins. At the very top was "vainglory," the sin of pride, from which he believed the other sins such as lust, envy and anger were born. Greed, gluttony, sloth, he considered small potatoes.

Unlike the biblically correct Ten Commandments, which focused on the very fabric of morality as well as respect for human life, the Seven Deadly Sins formed a category of minor vices that were, nonetheless, viewed as a slippery path down which the sinner could be assured of a relentless slide into evil. The most pitiful of these sinners were those who wore their transgression with the visibility of the chubby Michelin Man, and so were easy targets for the Church's relentless potshots. Sloth could be hidden behind closed doors; envy could be disguised as admiration tinged with just a hint of negativity. Greed could maintain its somewhat legitimate facade of ambition, but gluttony, because of its bloated nature, was an all-too-evident expansion of the waistline at the expense of the soul.

As the years fell away, so did the severity of the Church's responses to Gluttony and his six siblings. Instead of raining on its parishioners' picnic, why not focus, instead, on the behavior of monks within the confines of their cloistered, rarefied society? After all, their job description required them to practice a selfless dedication to God. The fly in the monastic soup turned out to be that medieval monasteries were not only dedicated to God but also to the overflowing wine goblet and the groaning board. Somehow, the monks managed to conduct the good works of the Church with the rollicking abandon of a never-ending Bar Mitzvah. From the look of their bulging robes, it was all too apparent that fasting and deprivation were a matter of somewhat loose religious interpretation.

"Gluttons dig their graves with their teeth."
—*GERMAN PROVERB*

"Temptations can be got rid of.
How?
By yielding to them."
—HONORÉ DE BALZAC

SACRED CHOW

During the Middle Ages the richest of the monasteries became the settings for the Church's most sumptuous entertaining. Most of the wine of their vineyard grapes filled not only the cup of the abbot but those of his esteemed guests as well. To best display the bounty that God had provided, huge banquets were mounted not only to celebrate the endless feast days that punctuated the Church's calendar but also to honor visiting religious and royal dignitaries. Even if the accepted propaganda flowing from the abbey was that devotion to one's belly was an ungodly waste of time, the nonstop gustatory reveling taking place within its great halls rivaled the culinary orgies of old Rome. All in all, the sin of gluttony became a lot less deadly as practiced by those who could whisper regularly into the ear of the Almighty.

Today, gluttony is often regarded by a more sympathetic society, as are most other characterological flaws, as a psychological problem with labels such as compulsive eating disorder, low self-esteem, obsessive or masochistic behavior. The slavish worship of the id has replaced many of the Church's favorite taboos. Sin, as Thomas Aquinas knew it, no longer requires a serious talk with your rabbi or priest, just a trip to your local library, which is filled to the rafters with self-help books. Written by legions of mental health professionals, they are dedicated to changing the old-time sinner into a New Age saint. On the other hand, gluttony may be viewed as a harmless overindulgence, to be cured not by soul-searching but by the occasional dose of Pepcid AC. And so, gentle reader, no matter how you choose to respond to the least sinful of the Seven Deadly Sins, there can be no doubt that gluttony is the one that best represents the ongoing joys of conspicuous consumption.

"He who has only coarse food to eat
and water to drink...
will, without looking for it,
find happiness."
—CONFUCIUS

Vatican kitchen detail from *Opéra* by Bartolomeo Scarpi, chef of Pope Pius V, Venice, 1596

Overleaf: *The Wedding at Cana*, 1563, by Paolo Veronese

BIRTHRIGHT POTTAGE

1 (3 ½ pound) chicken
2 cans (46-ounce) chicken broth,
   or 12 cups homemade broth
3 tablespoons olive oil
2 carrots, diced
About 1 pound (3 or 4, depending on size)
   potatoes, diced
½ cup dry lentils, preferably yellow

1 rutabaga or turnip, diced (use half if
   rutabaga is large)
1 medium onion, chopped
2 leeks, carefully washed and chopped
1 preserved lemon,* finely chopped,
   or juice of 1 lemon
Salt and pepper to taste

———

*Traditional preserved lemons must be made a month ahead. But Paula Wolfert offers a quicker version in *Couscous and Other Good Foods from Morocco*: With a razor blade, make 8 fine 2-inch vertical incisions in the peel around each lemon. (Do not cut deeper than the membrane that protects the pulp.) Place incised lemons in a stainless-steel saucepan with plenty of salt and water to cover and boil until peels become very soft. Place in a clean jar, cover with cooled cooking liquor, and leave to pickle for approximately 5 days. Unlike the 30-day lemons, these lemons will not keep up to a year, or even very long, but are perfectly acceptable if used soon.

TO POACH CHICKEN: Place in a large stockpot, cover with broth, preferably homemade (add water if you do not have enough broth). Bring to boil, immediately lower heat and simmer until chicken meat is falling off the bones.

Using tongs, lift chicken pieces out of pot and set aside to cool. When cool enough to handle, remove meat from bones. Shred chicken meat and pour a little broth over it and store, covered, in refrigerator until ready to use. (If using canned broth, return skin and bones to pot and simmer for an hour longer to enrich flavor.)

Strain broth through a sieve into a container, discard skin and bones, and refrigerate broth overnight, or until it is chilled enough so that all the fat has risen to the top. Remove fat and discard. Set broth aside.

TO MAKE POTTAGE: Heat olive oil in a large stockpot. Add diced carrots, potatoes and lentils, then rutabaga and finally onion and leeks. After each vegetable is added, stir it around to coat with oil and pan-roast for a few minutes. (This makes a real difference to the flavor of the pottage.)

Add 8 cups of broth (or add enough water to the broth to make 8 cups) and 1 to 2 teaspoons of salt, bring to a boil and simmer about $1/2$ hour, until vegetables are tender. Using a potato masher, mash some of the vegetables slightly to thicken pottage. If soup is too thick, add water to achieve desired consistency. Taste for seasoning; add salt, if needed.

Add reserved chicken and preserved lemon, or lemon juice, simmer gently for 20 minutes. Makes 10 servings.

A lesson on abstention.

Scripture Cake

1 ¹/2 cups chopped dried figs (Nahum 3:12)
2 ¹/4 cups water (Judges 4:19)
1 cup softened butter (Psalms 55:21)
2 cups sugar (Jeremiah 6:20)
2 tablespoons honey (Exodus 3:8)
6 eggs (Isaiah 10:14)
3 ³/4 cups flour (Leviticus 24:5)
1 teaspoon salt (II Kings 2:20)
3 teaspoons baking powder (AMOS 4:5)

1 teaspoon baking soda
1 tablespoon cinnamon (Revelation 18:13)
2 teaspoons ginger (I KINGS 10:2)
¹/2 teaspoon ground cloves
1 teaspoon nutmeg
1 cup milk (Genesis 18:8)
1 ³/4 cups chopped almonds (Numbers 17:8)
1 ¹/2 cups raisins (I Samuel 30:12)

Preheat oven to 300 degrees. Grease and flour a 10-cup Bundt pan.

In a small saucepan, simmer figs and water over medium-low heat until figs are very soft, about 20 minutes. Let cool.

In an electric mixer bowl, cream together butter and sugar until light and fluffy. Add honey. Then add eggs, one at a time, beating after each addition. Mix until well blended.

Puree cooled figs and water until smooth. Strain puree through triple cheese-cloth to Yield about a cup of fig essence.

In a separate bowl, sift together flour, salt, baking powder, baking soda and spices. Combine fig essence with milk, and alternately mix fig milk and dry ingredients with egg mixture, ending with the dry mixture. Fold in chopped almonds and raisins.

Pour batter into prepared pan and bake 1 hour and 35 minutes, or until toothpick inserted in center comes out with just a few crumbs on it. Cool for 20 minutes and then remove from pan and cool completely on cake rack. Makes 16 servings.

FABULOUS

FEASTS

As we eat our way back in history, no community is as famous as ancient Rome for setting a sybaritic table. Of all the civilizations credited with nonstop, culinary overkill, Rome should be awarded the "Order of the Gluttonous Maximus." As it grew ever richer in gold and slaves, the upper crust of Roman society began to entertain in the most lavish of ways in order to keep up with the Joneicuses next door. Any excuse was an acceptable reason to invite a few hundred people over for dinner. Popular occasions were sacrifices to the gods to ensure one's good fortune or success in love.

The most outrageous of the revelers were the emperors themselves, who celebrated their numerous victories by setting the most extraordinary tables in all of Rome. Julius Caesar was known to have thrown a royal feed for over 260,000 hungry Romans, who were served by 20,000 even hungrier slaves. The servers struggled valiantly to keep upright under heroic platters of eggs, artichokes, leeks, fish, roasts, fresh truffles, olives, oysters, shrimp, snails, pâtés—and those were only a few of the main courses.

As for hors d'oeuvres—along with braised camel's heels, hummingbird tongues and elephant ears, was a delicacy that today would be considered a choice nibble for Garfield: the tiniest of dormice bathed in fragrant oils and herbs.

If that were not enough

Un Sompteux Banquet au Palazzo Quirinale pour l'ambassadeur d'Angleterre en 1087

to make any self-respecting gladiator's mouth water, the grand finale of this endless parade of questionable concoctions was often a large roasted peacock, stuffed with quail, pigeon and a bushel or two of sea snails. Before the bird was presented to its eager audience, its plumage was carefully sewn back in place and its comb was gilded for a more dramatic entrance. No matter how caring the host, there seemed to be no effort to make a hypo-allergenic peacock for those who suffered from sensitivity to feathers.

Fortunately, there were enough leftovers to make two or three hundred peacock sandwiches. Those were put aside for the next night's entertainment of the host's "B" list guests, who were more than grateful for the scraps of the rich and famous.

CHEAPER BY THE DOZEN

Meanwhile, yet another legion of slaves, who had been confiscated from their native lands as the spoils of war, were cooking up a storm behind the scenes. They were the army of chefs who catered for Caesar's nearest and dearest. The head chef of a really successful banquet was almost certain to become an overnight star and be rewarded with riches and, finally, the freedom to open his own restaurant. Sound familiar?

Yet in those days, good chefs were a *sesterce* a dozen and a really noble Roman couldn't be expected to live by hummingbird tongues alone. The tableware fashions of the day were designed to echo the extravagance of the food. Nero was fond of having the movable ceiling above his table tipped to release millions of flower petals that would float down and cover not only the food but the guests, as well. The tables were made of ivory, gold or silver and encrusted with precious stones. They were laid with finely woven linen tablecloths and napkins, gem-studded blown-glass goblets and solid gold spoons. Since forks and table knives were things of the future, the Romans depended upon their hands for something as important as dining.

With the fall of the Roman Empire, the finer things in life, such as elegant table accouterments, disappeared. The barbarian hordes, who swept over Europe, had little use for monogrammed napkins.

Nevertheless, while the good times rolled, Roman hospitality included not only the pleasure of setting a luxurious table but also the pride the guests took in eating beyond the point of no return. But, in fact, there was a return of a somewhat explosive nature in a room specially set aside for ridding oneself of one's previous menu choices. These beautifully tiled but understandably sparsely furnished rooms were known as vomitoria. Every fine house had one and they were considered to be as important a sign of affluence as today's chic little powder room. The only way to insure that the Roman guest could survive until the end of the feast, with its mind-boggling number of courses, was to make room for more food in the fastest and most efficient way.

A really well-trained servant was all too familiar with the fine art of throat-tickling. Nero was known to have successfully participated in a thirty-six-hour banquet by bringing most of it up almost as fast as he scarfed it down. He was able to keep up the pace with the help of his personal physician, who periodically introduced the imperial feather down the imperial gullet.

Seneca, who was respected not only as a Roman senator but also as one of the Eternal City's leading party animals noted: *"vomunt et edunt, edunt et vomunt"* or "vomit and eat, eat and vomit." Perhaps not the kind of advice Emily Post might offer to those who are contemplating how best to impress their in-laws, but when in Rome...

The noblest citizens in town, after an exhausting day of chariot racing, slave trading and gladiator baiting, expanded their voluptuous dining habits into longer and longer evenings of non-stop gorging. The nobility played "Can You Top This?" with the most exotic foods in the empire. Cleopatra, in that faraway backwater known as Egypt, found that a crushed pearl dissolved in her wine made a nifty aperitif.

The banquet menu here, chronicled in the *Satyricon* of Petronius, would perhaps not be an instant "yum" for the cocktail crowd of today, but for Roman bon vivants, an invitation to it was one of the hottest tickets in town.

Hors d'oeuvres

Black and white olives

Dormice, sprinkled with poppy seeds and honey

Sausages with plums and pomegranate seeds

Pastry eggs stuffed with garden warblers

Beans, beefsteak, testicles and kidneys, sow's udder, lobster, bulls' eyes, one horned fish, one goose, two mullets (set on huge trays arranged in the shapes of the signs of the Zodiac)

Main Courses

Wild boar stuffed with wild thrushes served with cakes made in the shape of piglets

Syrian dates and grapes

Pigs stuffed with sausages and blood pudding made from boiled calf

Apples stuffed with powdered saffron

Afters

Pastry thrushes stuffed with raisins and nuts

Quinces studded with thorns to resemble sea urchins

Pork molded in the form of a goose, surrounded by fish and game

Various shellfish including snails

ANOTHER OPENING, ANOTHER SHOW

At the end of Banquet Number I, the guests would bathe and change clothing before attempting Banquet Number II, which was usually laid in a different dining room. This was probably done to avoid having annoying crumbs and half-chewed carcasses interfere with the rhythm of the second feast. The host had the daunting responsibility of keeping his guests not only stuffed to their formidable capacities but also amused. Enter the parasite. The appearance of

Let the Roman orgy begin: a toga party as imagined in *Quo Vadis*, 1951, MGM.

the parasite at banquets was one of the more important Roman social institutions. The custom of having a parasite, who made the guests laugh, and praised the host in exchange for an invitation to the feast, was handed down from the Greeks. Today, he might be called a stand-up comedian.

Aside from the talents of the parasite, and a procession of sugar-coated sweetmeats and honey-dipped pastries, there was also X-rated entertainment for dessert. As the art of the banquet evolved, Roman society decided that after-dinner mints were to be replaced by after-dinner orgies—the historic beginnings of the world's very first Toga Parties.

HIDING THE MATZOH

While the Romans were fanatically feasting, far from Party Central, Judea's Roman governor, Pontius Pilate, was heeding the rumors of a more intimate supper that was about to take place right under his patrician nose. Even though it was held in secret and attended by only a handful of people—in fact it was dinner for just twelve—it turned out to be the most significant feast the world would ever know. Jesus and His apostles, although often represented as sitting around the table for the Passover meal, likely reclined on couches in the accepted Roman style. The simple tablecloth that was covered with unleavened bread that night is represented today by the cloth that drapes the altar in Christian churches.

Monk-y Business

When the glory that was Rome disappeared from the landscape so did the glory of the formal banquet. It wasn't until the Dark Ages began to brighten up a bit that gastronomic fun and games became a major part of life once again. The nonstop revelry of the late Middle Ages, often under the auspices of the Church, included celebratory feasts that lasted for weeks. Chewing the fat was the entertainment of choice not only for the top clergy, but also for royals and rich landowners who sometimes entertained hundreds at a time at tables that should have buckled under the weight of the food.

A dozen kinds of meat and just as many fish courses, as well as scores of side dishes and an endless parade of exotic delicacies, were brought with great ceremony from a kitchen the size of a football field. During the course of the feast, spectacular sugar sculptures would be carried out from the kitchen and marched around the table. The prospect of an irresistible dessert was part of the inspiration that made it possible to eat the reeking meat and game that had been hanging around the larder long enough to apply for Social Security.

"Strange to see how a good dinner and feasting reconciles everybody."
—SAMUEL PEPYS

"I have never been anything so refined as a gourmet.
I am happy to say that I'm still capable of being a glutton."
—G. K. CHESTERTON

The Party's Never Over

No matter how inedible the food might have been at these giant snack-ins, eating was one of the few forms of diversion for most of medieval society. If a squire acquired enough money for a life of privilege, the sad truth was that there was almost nothing to spend it on except feeding himself and a few hundred close, personal friends. The only occupation that rivaled that of the kitchen worker was that of the tailor, who spent most of his time letting out his customers' robes.

Things went from bad to wurst and so, in the 14th century, Edward II approved laws to keep his subjects from eating themselves out of castle and home. The Sumptuary Laws made it an offense of the most serious nature to exceed one's income to entertain lavishly. It's likely that Edward's laws were digested with the same relish that his subjects showed for a really terrific rabbit pudding, and then promptly ignored.

Edward III had the same dubious success in enforcing the laws as his predecessor, and finally, when Richard II took over at the head of the royal table, entertaining hit a new high. On one evening he invited more than 10,000 guests, as 2,000 cooks spoiled the broth, aided by 300 servers. The specialties du jour included fourteen whole oxen, 120 head of sheep, twelve boars, fourteen calves, 140 pigs, three tons of salted venison, 50 swans, 210 geese, 100 dozen pigeons, 60 dozen hens, 100 gallons of milk and 11,000 eggs.

And that was only for the afternoon sitting. Clearly, things had gotten out of hand.

Red Snails in the Sunset

After the Age of Exploration dawned, there were whole new continents for Europeans to explore and conquer. Eventually, the busy populace found it necessary to excuse itself from the table.

One of the last spectacular examples of a dinner fit for a king was the intimate little party thrown by Louis XVIII in 1816 for 10,000 members of the military. It was held under tents that extended from the Place de la Concorde all the way to the Étoile. Antonin Carême was one of a hundred chefs who served up a carnivore's delight lacking only four and twenty blackbirds baked in a pie. Carême, a chef of few words, was heard to gasp, "Never was work more agonizing for the cooks."

Hail to the Chef

As appetites were being trimmed in Europe, Americans began to discover the joys of cooking in a democratic society. In 1800, that dedicated Francophile, Thomas Jefferson was elected President. Jefferson brought his devotion to French cuisine into the White House, then called "The President's House." The time Jefferson had spent in Paris polished his love of fine food and wine, which he loved to share with guests whenever possible. He brought his accomplished French chef and French steward to oversee his cosmopolitan dinner parties in Washington. However,

Les Noces Alsaciennes by
Paul Kaufmann

since Jefferson regard-
ed formality and rigid
protocol as hindrances
to hospitable enter-
taining, he used a
round table for dinner
parties so that his
guests would feel
equally important in
his company. Aside
from being a great president, Jefferson was a truly gracious host.

In the 1880s, another true gourmet influenced U.S. politics. Sam Ward was an important mover and shaker in Washington who both advised President Rutherford Hayes on political matters and stirred up the White House kitchen with his menus for formal dinners. Since
the young country's culinary inferiority complex was a consideration, Ward's typical *carte du jour*
had more French in it than Maurice Chevalier. The nineteen resplendent courses served at one
state dinner proved how far the New World had come from that first turkey and succotash social
that a group of overdressed Pilgrims shared with the Wampanoag, their brand-new friends, who
had a much more relaxed dress code.

FROM *LES FASTES DE BACCHUS ET COMUS* BY G. OBERLE, NEW YORK
ACADEMY OF MEDICINE LIBRARY

I'll Have the Foie Gras, Please

Time marches on and in 1975, one of America's most respected food writers, Craig Claiborne, restaurant critic for *The New York Times*, was offered the opportunity to orchestrate a dinner for two, and to create the menu of his dreams, at a restaurant anywhere in the world. Claiborne immediately ruled out his local Pizza Hut and opted, instead, for the hautest

of haute cuisine at Chez Denis in Paris. He took with him as his "second fork" Pierre Franey, himself a world-famous chef. Aside from its superb cuisine, Chez Denis was known for having tossed out the Michelin inspectors, after being informed that they would award it three stars if the owner would just clean the place up. Never let it be said that Claiborne permitted a well-vacuumed rug to be the determinant of his choice of tummy temples.

Clearly he made the right decision,

since the extraordinary banquet that was put before him was in his estimation worth every penny of the four-thousand dollar bill, tip included. That sum might not turn a head in today's inner-sanctums of gastronomy but in 1975 it was billed as the world's most expensive meal. The menu was given in *The New York Times*.

"I hate people who are not serious about their meals."
—OSCAR WILDE

Overleaf: *The Christening Feast,* 1664, by Jan Steen

Hors Service
Beluga Caviar

Premier Service
Consommé Denis
Cream of Sorrel Soup
Tomato Soup with pimento and herbs
Individual tarts with ham, mushrooms and truffles
Parfait of Sweetbreads
Tarts of Quail Mousse
Belon Oysters served in a beurre blanc
Lobster au Gratin
Rougets (red mullet), done in a pie with tomato and olives
Bresse chickens in cream with wild mushrooms
Roast Partridge with cabbage
Filet of Beef in a truffle sauce

Second Service
Ortolans (tiny birds eaten in one bite) en brochette
Filets of wild ducks
Loin of veal in puff pastry
Pommes Anna
Puree of fresh artichokes
Baked sliced potatoes with black truffle
Foie Gras in aspic
Breast of woodcock in aspic
Cold sliced pheasant in aspic

Third Service
Floating Island
Poires Alma

Mme. Lemozy's Roasted Stuffed Lamb

1 shoulder of lamb,* boned, 4 to 6 pounds
1 pound ground pork
1 egg
2 or 3 cloves garlic, finely minced
1/4 cup minced fresh parsley
1 teaspoon fresh marjoram, minced
1 teaspoon fresh thyme, minced
2 teaspoons salt, or to taste
1 teaspoon freshly ground pepper
1/2 cup unseasoned bread crumbs
Fines herbes: equal parts minced chervil, parsley, chives and tarragon, to make 1/2 cup
8 tomatoes, halved

---

*If you can't find a butcher who will bone a shoulder of lamb (comparable to a chuck roast of beef), a leg of lamb may be substituted, but it may not be quite as succulent.

Mix together well: pork, egg, garlic, parsley, marjoram, thyme, salt, pepper and bread crumbs. Make a small patty of the pork mixture and fry it to taste for seasoning. Adjust seasoning. Spread evenly over the lamb. Roll up the meat and tie with string.

Place in a deep, oval, buttered casserole dish or roasting pan and roast in a 425-degree oven for 1 to 1 1/2 hours, or until the internal temperature of the roast reaches 150 to 155 degrees. Sprinkle water on the meat from time to time.

After about 30 minutes of cooking, sprinkle with salt and pepper and *fines herbes*. During the last half-hour of cooking, arrange tomatoes around the meat and sprinkle with salt and pepper. When meat is cooked, remove string, carve, and serve hot, surrounded by tomatoes. Sprinkle with more *fines herbes*. Makes 8 servings.

ROYAL FILET
OF BEEF

Prepare and prick a large filet of Normandy beef, place it on a large oval dish and pour over it a glass of Aix olive oil, a large onion chopped, branches of parsley, a bay leaf cut in four and a large, grated peppercorn. After three or four hours, pour off the marinade. pierce it lengthwise with a skewer attached to the spit, cover it with oiled paper and place it in front of the fire and moisten it with oil. Three quarters of an hour later, remove the paper, so as to dry the fat and color it blond. Five minutes before serving glaze it.

—Antonin Carême's recipe for *Filet de Boeuf Pique à la Broche.*

We've made only slight changes to this dish created for royal consumption at the Brighton Pavilion. Nowadays, we refrigerate marinating meat and we assume that it will be cooked in a home oven.

═══════

1 (3-pound) filet of beef, trimmed and tied
3/4 cup olive oil
1 large onion, chopped
1/4 cup chopped fresh parsley
1 bay leaf, torn into fourths
Freshly ground pepper

═══════

In a medium bowl, mix oil, onion, parsley, bay leaf and a generous grinding of pepper. Place beef filet in a large, oval dish and pour marinade over it. Turn to coat on all sides. Cover and refrigerate for at least 3 or 4 hours. Turn once while marinating. After filet has marinated, place it on a rack in a roasting pan. Spoon some of the parsley and onions from marinade on top of filet, draining off as much oil as possible. Roast in preheated 475-degree oven for about 45 minutes. For medium rare, remove filet from oven when an instant-read thermometer registers 120 degrees. Allow meat to sit for 10 to 15 minutes. The temperature will continue to rise 5 to 10 degrees, bringing it to medium rare. Makes 6 servings.

Carême served it with creamy mashed potatoes. It's also fit for a prince when accompanied by roasted red potatoes.

DUCK BREASTS IN WINE

This recipe uses almost 2 bottles of red wine, but the intense flavor is worth it. Drink the rest.

FOR DUCK:
5 cups red wine, such as Merlot
2 whole duck breasts (about 2 pounds)
Salt and pepper

FOR MIREPOIX:
2 tablespoons rendered duck fat or butter
1 tablespoon olive oil
3/4 cup minced celery
3/4 cup minced carrot
1 medium onion, minced
1 bay leaf
1/2 teaspoon dried thyme

TO MAKE WINE GLAZE: In a saucepan, boil 4 cups red wine and reduce it to about 1/2 cup.

TO PREPARE DUCK: Trim tendons from duck breasts. Cut each breast in half, so that you have 4 pieces. Lay breasts on a cake rack, skin-side down. Set the rack over a baking pan and use pastry brush to paint some of the glaze on top of the breasts. (The pan is to catch and save any glaze that drips off.) Set aside for 1/2 hour at room temperature.

Pat pieces of breast dry and place them, skin-side down, in a heavy skillet, preferably cast iron. Sear over moderately high heat for 3 or 4 minutes, then turn and cook other side until lightly browned. Remove from pan and set aside.

When cool enough to handle, remove remaining skin and fat, which will pull away easily from the meat. Season both sides of the breasts with salt and pepper. Pour off rendered fat from skillet; it is highly prized and may be reserved for frying potatoes and other cooking uses.

TO PREPARE MIREPOIX: Heat duck fat or butter and olive oil in a skillet. Add minced celery and carrot, onion, bay leaf and thyme. Sauté over medium heat, stirring occasionally, until vegetables are soft, about 10 or 12 minutes. Set aside.

Deglaze pan using remaining glaze and remaining 1 cup of red wine. Add mirepoix. Cook briefly, then force sauce through a sieve or food mill. Return duck breasts to pan and heat gently until heated through and cooked

to taste. (For rare duck breasts, the cooking should be brief, as they are already pretty much cooked by the first searing.)

Slice each piece of breast thinly on a diagonal, arrange in fan shape on plate and spoon sauce over each serving. If there is any additional sauce, pass it on the side. Makes 4 servings.

MUSÉE CONDÉ, CHANTILLY

Detail from *Très Riches Hueres du Duc du Berri*

PARADISE POACHED PEARS

This elegant dessert of pears poached in port and topped with whipped cream was inspired by the dessert enjoyed by Craig Claiborne and Pierre Franey at their $4,000 dinner in Paris in 1975.

8 almond cookies, broken into pieces
8 ripe pears, still firm
Juice of ¹/2 lemon
4 cups water
1 cup port wine

1 ¹/4 cups sugar
1 small piece cinnamon stick
¹/2 orange rind, plus grated zest for garnish
1 strip of lemon peel
Cream for whipping

Preheat oven to 350 degrees. Place cookie pieces into a food processor and process to crumbs. Place crumbs on a baking sheet and bake for a few minutes until they are light brown and toasted. Watch carefully, so they do not burn. Cool and set aside.

Peel the pears, halve and place them into a bowl of cold water with the lemon juice. This will keep them from getting brown.

Combine the 4 cups of water with the rest of the ingredients, except cream, and bring the mixture to a boil, stirring to dissolve sugar completely.

Add the pears and simmer until the fruit is tender. Do not overcook. Let the pears cool in the liquid for about 15 minutes. Gently remove pears and place into a container and chill. Remove cinnamon stick, lemon peel and orange rind from liquid and return the liquid to heat. Bring it to a boil, reduce until syrupy. Cool.

Whip cream until soft peaks form.

Serve 2 pear halves on each dessert dish with syrup spooned over them. Add a dollop of whipped cream. Sprinkle toasted almond-cookie crumbs and orange zest over the top. Makes 8 servings.

CHAPTER THREE

HAUTE

BLOAT

Gluttony in today's society is much more than a sin, it's a one-way ticket to *Palookaville*. Pity the poor transgressor who dares to ask for seconds at a smart little dinner party or chooses the giant size popcorn at the movies. He or she is most certainly banished to the purgatory of the uninformed, the unhealthy and, most damning of all, the un-chic. Flaunting one's dedication to the bounty of the refrigerator by sporting a substantial layer of cellulite is a definite no-no with the movers and shakers who think that *Vogue* and *GQ* are not just hair-dryer entertainment, but mission statements on how to achieve a successful and happy life.

But that wasn't always the way the fine art of culinary overindulgence was viewed. In bygone days, your social status and wealth were often ascertained by your overfed profile. Excess body baggage signaled to the world that the size of your bank account was even bigger than your waistline.

In Old Rome, that rotund party thrower, Apicius, devoted his

The peacock, which belongs to the pheasant family, was a star dinner dish for two millennia.

vast fortune to keeping himself and his guests as well fed as possible. He was not only the host with the mostest but also the creator of the world's first cookbook or, at least, the oldest culinary manual that survives. It includes not only recipes but also remedies for stomachaches and other ills that came from living high on the Roman hog. Apicius, alas, came to an ignoble end when he found that he had spent most of his fortune on setting the finest table in all Rome. When he could no longer impress his fellow gluttons by lavishing food and wine upon them, he threw in the toga and committed suicide. You could say that Apicius was the world's first Roman ruin.

A Bird for All Seasons

The exalted head of the Roman Catholic Church is perhaps the last person you would expect to find wolfing down his daily bread but the Renaissance pope, Julius III, thought nothing of having several peacocks prepared for his midday meal. The story goes that since peacock was his favorite food and there was a whole one left after he had gobbled down the others at dinner, he asked that it be served cold after his evening prayers. To his horror, the peacock that arrived turned out to be freshly roasted and not the cold leftover of the pontiff's dreams. Trying to soothe the pope's very ruffled feathers, one of his cardinals said, "Let not your holiness, I pray you, be moved by a matter of such small weight."

Faster than a speeding drumstick, the pope replied, "If God were so angry for an apple that He cast our parents out of paradise, why may not I, His vicar, be angry then for a peacock, since a peacock is a greater matter than an apple?"

Fed Up With It All

GALLERIA NAZIONALE, ROME

The more you weighed in Tudor times the larger your fortune was perceived to be. As one can see from his portrait, for Henry VIII size definitely mattered. Aside from money, substantial girth was equated with heroic valor and was a sure sign that a man was to be taken seriously by his enemies. His body was meant to be an extension of his weaponry; the very sight of it was meant to both impress and overwhelm his opponent. Henry set about making himself into the world's most physically-formidable ruler. It was scarcely a problem for him since he worked up a considerable appetite beheading two of his seven wives. Overeating was one of his favorite pastimes aside from war and matrimony.

At a typical dinner, Henry could be counted on to polish off a whole joint of lamb, and reduce a small deer to a pile of polished bones. Then on to a pair of lobsters, several plovers, followed by calf's head pie; the meal topped off with enough gingerbread and quince tartlettes to feed all of his ex in-laws. By 1547, at the age of 56, he had to be carried from room to room because of his immense size. At the time of his death, his distended stomach could no longer be confined by his clothing, and the circumference of his chest measured almost sixty inches. The irony is that Henry VIII's very favorite food was the humble artichoke which has almost no calories.

On Éclair Day

In the 16th century, the French also exerted some very impressive culinary muscle. Henri IV, who typically picked his way through a dinner consisting of four plates of soup, a pheasant, a partridge, two slices of ham, a huge salad (for royal roughage, of course), a leg of mutton with garlic, pastry, fruit and several hard-boiled eggs, tried to enforce the sumptuary laws that Philippe IV had issued in the late 1200s, in the hope of protecting his subjects from a nationwide Edible Complex.

Unfortunately, King Henri missed the *bateau* when it came to convincing his subjects to cut back on their intake of cream puffs. The French ignored the laws with a Gallic wink, and why not, when the King himself took to adding a cup or two of pure gold along with precious gems to his menu. At the time it was believed that dining on gold could make you immortal, while rubies were thought to be a great tonic for decay, and sapphires were a surefire cure for ulcers. To add insult to corpulence, Henri IV, who was known for his equestrian talents, was such a prodigious eater that finally he had to be raised onto his horse with a mechanical lift, much to the dismay of not only his physicians but also his horse. After he was assassinated, it was discovered that Henri's stomach was almost five times the normal size.

My Kingdom for A Horse

Yet another royal stuffer was burdened not only with an insatiable case of the munchies but also with a rather tentative grasp of reality. Mad King Ludwig of Bavaria, as he was affectionately known by his people, ascended the throne in 1864, at age 19. By that time he had lost most of his teeth because of his crazy addiction to sweets. To make matters worse, he always dined alone even though he believed that his dinner guests included Louis XV and Louis' main squeeze, Madame de Pompadour. Before the servants had a chance to remove the untouched plates of Ludwig's invisible guests, he would eat their dinners as well as his own.

On evenings when his favorite guests were otherwise engaged haunting Versailles, Ludwig asked that his horse be brought from the stable to his table, giving new meaning to the phrase "putting on the feedbag." As was the case with King Louis and Madame de P., Ludwig ate the horse's untouched food with irrepressible gusto, which gave new meaning to the phrase, "right from the horse's mouth."

Truth is often stranger than fiction, but not always. Rabelais, the 16th-century French satirist, wrote a social comedy about two giants, Gargantua and his son Pantagruel, as a spoof of French mores. Their appetites were so enormous that they devoured almost anything that crossed their paths in the course of their fantastic adventures. When those two said that they "ate the whole thing," they were being absolutely accurate. One of their more indigestible exploits had to do with the slurping up by Gargantua of six hapless pilgrims who were hiding in a field of cabbages he had decided to use for his salad. Not unlike a handful of peanuts, the pilgrims lodged in the giant's teeth, and he was forced to drink gallons of water and then use a tree trunk as a toothpick to dislodge them.

The moment after the pilgrims were pried from his teeth, Garagantua found it necessary to relieve himself of the massive amounts of water he had just gulped down. The river he created in front of himself was used by the terrified pilgrims to float away to freedom. It would be safe to say that they were pissed about the whole episode.

"Never eat more than you can lift."
—MISS PIGGY

DIAMONDS ARE A BOY'S BEST FRIEND

One of the more sparkling gluttons at the turn of the last century was the flamboyant Diamond Jim Brady who, along with his habit of giving out exquisite diamond jewelry at the drop of a pinkie ring, was a legendary eater. He was referred to during his lifetime and beyond as "the greatest glutton in American history." It wasn't at all unusual for him to eat six times a day, or order seven or eight steaks at one sitting, or chew on forty ears of corn in the course of one meal.

He considered a light breakfast to consist of a thick porterhouse steak, several lamb chops, six scrambled eggs, a stack of buttermilk pancakes, a plate of hominy, home-fried potatoes, corn muffins and a gallon of milk.

During the course of every meal he downed two or three pitchers of freshly squeezed orange juice, perhaps because he considered alcohol bad for the digestion. Right after breakfast, Jim would stop in at a seafood house for three or four dozen oysters and clams on the half shell, as well as enough oyster stew to fill a small bathtub.

To Jim's great surprise, his orgiastic eating began to draw crowds. People came from all over just to watch him vacuum up a table laden with food. Not only did he march through all the courses with the dedication of Grant taking Richmond, but he would up the ante by doubling and tripling the helpings, then end the meal with a pound of assorted bonbons.

Brady cut an amazing figure of flash as well as rippling flesh. His extended waist was encircled by a thick alligator belt, buckled in flawless stones. His thick fingers were covered with four or five eye-popping diamond rings and his lapels were festooned with diamond-encrusted pins and emblems. On a lean man, perhaps, all those decorations might seem tawdry, but on Diamond Jim Brady they were the jewels in his crown.

"Wish I had time for just one more bowl of chili."
—*KIT CARSON, AS HE LAY DYING*

Fat is Beautiful

The award for the bravest of our world-class eaters goes to the present king of Tonga, Taufa'ahua Tupou IV, who until just recently was considered to be the world's heaviest monarch. He proudly tipped the Tongan scales at over 444 pounds, give or take. The natural state of most of the Tongan population is happy obesity. You could say, in Tonga, fat is beautiful.

It took the king's loyal, if rather hefty, subjects completely by surprise when he was bitten by the fitness bug, and decided to become a calorie counter, especially since the royal family has always been expected to be much larger in physical stature than the rest of their people. So far, the king has trimmed down to a svelte 300 and something pounds, and he has invested in a Royal Treadmill.

His resolve is commendable since he was forced to give up one of his favorite treats, fruit bats, a delicacy reserved for Tongan royalty. Commoners, inspired by his resolve, have vowed to cut back dramatically on yams, hams and coconuts. The King in his wisdom and generosity has offered to bestow a brand new vegetable steamer on each of his subjects who loses twenty pounds. In the not-too-distant future, Calista Flockhart might just be able to blend into the Tongan passing parade.

Right: Untitled #172, 1987, by Cindy Sherman

Overleaf: Illustration by Walter Crane from *This Little Pig Went to Market*, London: 1895. Frances Converse Massey Collection. Reprinted in *The Ubiquitous Pig* by Marilyn Nissenson & Susan Jonas.

Apicius' Asparagus Patina

Put in the mortar asparagus tips, pound, add wine, pass through the sieve. Pound pepper, lovage, fresh coriander, savory, onion, wine, liquamen and oil. Put puree and spices into a greased shallow pan, and if you wish, break eggs over it when it is on the fire, so that the mixture sets. Sprinkle finely-ground pepper over it and serve.
—Marcus Apicius, *De Re Coquinaria*, Book IV .

We adapted this noble first-century recipe for a dish similar to a frittata by substituting celery for lovage, salt for liquamen.

1 tablespoon oil
1/2 cup chopped celery
1/4 cup chopped onion
1/3 cup asparagus, cut into 1/2-inch pieces, leaving tips whole
6 eggs

3/4 teaspoon salt
Freshly ground pepper to taste
1/2 teaspoon dried savory
2 tablespoons chopped fresh cilantro, plus more for garnish

Heat oil in a large sauté pan over medium-high heat and sauté celery and onion until onion is translucent. Add asparagus, lower heat to medium-low, cover, and steam until asparagus is just tender, about 5 to 7 minutes.

Beat eggs with salt, pepper and herbs. Pour mixture into pan and cook on high until eggs are set. Sprinkle with more chopped cilantro. Makes 4 servings.

TRIPLE CROWN GINGERBREAD

"To make gingerbrede. Take goode honey & clarifye it on fere & take fayre paynemayn or wastel brede & grate it & caste it into boylenge hony, & stere it well togyder faste..."
—14TH CENTURY RECIPE FROM *CURYE ON INGLYSCHE*

---

2 eggs
1 (8-ounce) container sour cream
$^{1}/_{2}$ cup molasses
$^{1}/_{2}$ cup firmly packed brown sugar
1 $^{1}/_{2}$ cups cake flour, not self-rising
1 teaspoon baking soda

1 $^{1}/_{2}$ teaspoons powdered ginger
$^{1}/_{4}$ teaspoon salt
2 teaspoons grated fresh ginger
$^{1}/_{2}$ cup melted butter
$^{1}/_{4}$ cup chopped crystallized ginger

Preheat oven to 350 degrees. Butter a 9-inch square pan.

Beat eggs until light in color. Add sour cream, molasses and brown sugar; mix well.

In a separate bowl, sift together cake flour, baking soda, powdered ginger and salt. Add to the egg mixture. Stir well, then mix in fresh ginger. Add the melted butter and beat well. Finally, fold in the crystallized ginger.

Pour into the prepared pan and bake for 30 minutes, or until toothpick comes out clean. Makes 12 servings.

Diamond Jim Oyster Stew

This simple, but incredibly rich dish can be modified to your own taste by adding more oysters or Tabasco sauce. Indulge yourself by purchasing oysters that have already been shucked.

---

1 pound shucked oysters with liquor
³/4 cup half-and-half
³/4 cup heavy cream
About 5 dashes Tabasco sauce, or to taste

Salt to taste
White pepper to taste
4 tablespoons butter
Paprika for garnish

Drain oyster liquor from the shucked oysters and reserve.

In a saucepan, combine half-and-half, heavy cream and oyster liquor and heat over medium-low heat. (If there is more than a cup of liquor, you may not want to use all of it. Start with a cup and then add to taste.)

Add Tabasco, salt and pepper. When cream is very hot, but not simmering, add the oysters. They will cook very quickly. They are done when the edges have begun to curl. Place 1 tablespoon of butter in each bowl before serving. Ladle equal amounts of oysters and broth into each bowl. Sprinkle with paprika. Makes 4 servings.

Serve with buttered toast or oyster crackers.

CRABMEAT CHASSEUR

This luxurious recipe comes from a 1950s handwritten card in the recipe collection of food writer Bernadette Wheeler. It's a gift from a time when prices were low and calorie counts high.

3 tablespoons butter
4 to 5 large mushrooms, sliced (about ³/4 cup)
3 teaspoons finely chopped shallots
2 tablespoons tomato puree
1 ¹/4 cup heavy cream, divided
1 pound fresh crabmeat, preferably jumbo lump

Salt and pepper to taste
1 ¹/2 teaspoons chopped parsley
1 teaspoon chopped fresh tarragon or ¹/2 teaspoon dried
1 teaspoon chopped fresh chives
2 egg yolks
Generous dash of cognac

Melt butter in saucepan, add mushrooms and cook for 5 minutes. Add shallots, stir and cook until almost all of the mushroom liquid has evaporated.

Add puree and cook 5 minutes more. Pour in 1 cup of the cream, stir and cook until thoroughly blended and mixture starts to thicken.

Gently add crabmeat and season to taste. (Use folding motion to combine crabmeat so the large pieces don't break up.)

Mix egg yolks with remaining 1/4 cup cream and add to crabmeat with herbs, again using folding motion to mix. Heat until slightly thickened. Add cognac.

Serve on rice or with toast points. Makes an extravagant first course for 4 or main course for 2.

CHAPTER FOUR

BACCHUS

TO THE
FUTURE

Anyone who thinks that gluttony has only to do with the abandonment of all restraint when it comes to food, probably never worshipped at the feet of the grapevine deity, Bacchus, in all his besotted glory. Long before the dawn of the Christian world, the most glamorous orgies of the Greek and Roman haut monde were fueled by the luscious fruit of his vine. And, predating those giddy days, the Mesopotamians, the Babylonians and the Egyptians were brewing their own drink of choice, beer.

Beer dates back, at least, to 6000 B.C. Since Mesopotamia was where civilization began, you'd think the Mesopotamians would have been too busy setting down the ground rules for civility to jot beer recipes in cuneiform, but that's just what they did. Their beer was made from barley (or other cereals), fermented with honey; for extra pizzazz, herbs and spices were added. The Egyptians modernized the brew into a more recognizable draft with the addition of hops and yeast.

Way north and later on, the Anglo-Saxons were bellying up to a different bar where the libation called mead was served. Mead, similar to beer, is made from the fermentation of honey and water, with spices added. This sweet beverage characteristically had an alcohol content of about 8 per cent. Conquering Romans referred to the brew as hydromel or honey-water.

Mead remained popular for centuries but had virtually disappeared by the end of the 1800s as beer grew in favor throughout Europe. Beer was consumed most often as a breakfast beverage and was the most common breakfast drink for most northern Europeans until well into the 19th century—long before the invention of the six-pack or the Super Bowl.

"I like the taste of beer, its live white lather, its bright-brass depths, the sudden world through the wet-brown walls of the glass, the tilted rush to the lips and slow swallowing down to the lapping belly, the salt on the tongue, the foam at the corners."
—DYLAN THOMAS

DAZE OF WINE AND ROSES

The Romans, who were famous for their grape expectations when it came to putting on a first class bacchanal, spared no expense in serving an astonishing amount of the "nectar of the gods" during the course of an evening. In summer, wine was served chilled; in winter, it was gently heated.

Even though wine was customarily mixed with water in those days, it packed a patrician punch. The best way to be welcomed into the Emperor Tiberius' inner circle was to drink enough fruit of the vine to make you almost incoherent, which was just the way he liked most of his closest friends. Gluttony, when it came to the grape, meant your political career in the senate or as a member of the emperor's household would advance with the speed of the latest model chariot.

Venus, Cupid, Bacchus, and Ceres by Cornelis van Haarlem (1562-1638)

The Romans weren't satisfied to keep their dipsomania to themselves. They planted vineyards wherever they made a conquest; before long the rest of Europe was rolling out the barrel with Latin dedication.

After the fall of the Roman Empire led to that bleak period known as the Dark Ages, the Church became the vintners of record. The monks and friars who filled the huge monasteries all over Europe used wine not only for religious purposes but also to keep their strength up between services. Having a nip or two escalated into the formal assembly of a serious wine cellar, complete with cellar master. Liquid overindulgence was part of the outrageous banquets that took place in the name of God. After a while it was hard to tell just which god was being worshipped.

Some monasteries even had their own private-label, rare cognacs. Spirits were made from fruits such as quince or plum. For medical remedies, wines were infused with herbs, conveniently giving them a whole new profile identified with healing rather than outright pleasure. There were even pharmacological monks who advised their patients to get drunk once a month, religiously, to maintain a good level of health. Thus began the alibi, "I drink, but only for medicinal purposes."

It's a Bird, It's a Plane, It's Super Grape

In the 17th century, one of the more successful of the holier-than-thou bunch was a shy Benedictine monk named Dom Pierre Perignon, cellar master at the Abbey of Hautvillers, who in his spare time experimented with blending different grape juices. Little did he know it then, but "it tickles my nose" was a phrase that would be heard for centuries to come. His juicy little experiment encouraged a special blend of grapes, when corked, to produce a carbonation that was to launch a thousand ships. It ultimately caused such a sensation in France that a special glass was molded around Marie Antoinette's breast (as uncomfortable as that sounds) to be used just for sipping Le Dom's heavenly brew.

"Come quickly, I am tasting the stars."
—DOM PERIGNON

VINTAGE VIRTUOSOS

When the French began their love affair with fine cuisine, great chefs such as Carême and Escoffier began to choose appropriate wines to accompany the various courses of a formal dinner. As the menu grew so did the consumption of wine, and overfed diners often left the table in a state of inebriation. Unlike socially unacceptable gluttony, a preoccupation with the grape was indulged as an appreciation of the good life.

Even today, with aggressive 12-step programs and enough books on substance abuse to fill the Library of Congress, consuming large quantities of fine wines is unlikely to raise a single eyebrow, but instead will win the drinker the respect given to a bonafide oenophile.

During the early 1900s, a rumor started in Paris that a man could perform much better sexually if he were half drunk. Needless to say, the wine merchants of the city were très ecstatic, while the local boulevardiers were higher than the Eiffel Tower. As we start the new century, the French are still knocking back about thirty-five gallons of wine each per year, and that doesn't include les enfants who are just learning to mix Chateau Latour with their Ovaltine.

Set 'Em Up, Joe

It's hard to believe that London, in the land of the stiff upper lip, was the setting of a rather extraordinary display of excess in the name of the noble grape. It took place in 1997, at that darling of the Michelin set, Le Gavroche, known almost as well for its rare wine collection as its cuisine. A dinner for four, hosted by Viktor Kozeny, a Czech multimillionaire fondly called "The Pirate of Prague" by people unfortunate enough to have had business dealings with him, cost, in British sterling, the equivalent of more than $21,000.

Black Rum and Other Vices, 1997, by Graham Knuttel

COURTESY OF APOLLO GALLERY, DUBLIN

Kozeny ordered a meal for his guests that was simple enough to almost have been mistaken for spa cuisine, with nary a truffle in sight, but the choice of the wines which accompanied it would make even Baron Rothschild rosé with envy. Kozeny began modestly with a bottle of 1949 Krug champagne ($929). Lobster mousse and *saumon en papillote* were accompanied by a fine white Burgundy ($2,324).

As the wait staff stood off in a corner calculating what the tip might amount to, there was a signal from the table that all was not well. The Pirate of Prague was upset. Having tasted the bottle of Burgundy ($8,300) he had ordered for the meat course, he found it unacceptable. A hush came over the entire restaurant as everyone held their collective breath, waiting to see if a young virgin might have to be sacrificed to appease the pirate.

Astonishingly, the pirate just went on to order another bottle, this time a Bordeaux, a 1945 Haut Brion ($3,486). For the dessert omelets, Kozeny chose a 1967 d'Yquem, which was a steal at $1,776. Brandies at $332 per snifter, and enough cigars to keep even Monica Lewinsky happy, rounded out this colossal display of excess.

After the check was handed to the Czech, his response was to make a reservation for the following week. Reports of his next dinner were that the bill came to a very subdued $13,280. The pirate must have switched to Thunderbird.

"The whole world is about three drinks behind."
—*HUMPHREY BOGART*

Overleaf: *The Topers*, 1628, by Diego Velásquez

Star-Sparkle Champagne Punch

1 bottle white Burgundy
1/2 cup brandy
1/4 cup orange-flavored liqueur
1/2 cup lemon juice
3 tablespoons sugar
1 lime, sliced

1 lemon, sliced
1/2 orange, sliced
1 pint strawberries, sliced
1 bottle extra-dry champagne
1/2 quart club soda

Mix together Burgundy, brandy, orange-flavored liqueur, lemon juice and sugar in a 2-quart container. Add sliced lime, lemon, orange and strawberries to mixture. Refrigerate for several hours or overnight to allow flavors to meld.

When ready to serve, put ice or an ice mold in a punch bowl. Pour in 1/2 of the Burgundy mixture, the bottle of champagne and the club soda. (Keep the unused half of the Burgundy mixture for the next batch of punch.) Makes 12 servings.

ALPHONSE MUCHA, 1897

GILDED CHOCOLATE COGNAC TRUFFLES

Gluttony may be a sin, but patience is a virtue. These extravagant beauties require a great deal of care and time, but are well worth it. Although you will not use the entire package of gold leaf, you may need extra sheets to practice with when you make these truffles for the first time because the fragile sheets tear easily.

———

36 ounces high-quality semisweet chocolate, divided
12 ounces high-quality bittersweet chocolate, divided
1 1/2 cups heavy cream
3 tablespoons cognac
5 tablespoons unsalted butter, softened
1 1/2 teaspoons solid vegetable shortening
1 package 3-inch-square, 23-carat edible gold leaf, about 25 leaves

———

In a double boiler, melt 20 ounces of semisweet and 4 ounces of bittersweet chocolate over hot, not boiling, water. Once melted, turn off the heat.

In a small saucepan, heat heavy cream just until it reaches the boiling point. Whisk the cream into the melted chocolate. Place the saucepan in the refrigerator for about 10 min-utes to cool. Remove and beat in the cognac and butter. Transfer mixture into a bowl and refrigerate for 3 or 4 hours, or until firm.

Using the large end of a melon baller, scoop out some of the mixture to form uneven-ly shaped balls. Keep a bowl of very hot water next to the work area to occasionally warm the melon baller. This will make the scooping a bit easier, but be sure to dry the melon baller thoroughly before touching the chocolate mixture. Place the balls on 2 wax-paper lined baking sheets. As each sheet becomes full, place in the refrigerator for about 10 minutes to firm up. Then remove from refrigerator and with clean hands roll each ball to shape and smooth. Place the balls on a freshly lined baking sheet and return to the refrigerator.

TO PREPARE THE GOLD LEAF: Make sure everything is very dry and the windows are shut. The smallest breeze will make the sheets fold over themselves. Each piece of gold leaf is on a piece of tissue. Prepare the gold leaf by using a scissors to cut a few of the sheets together. Cut into quarters very carefully; the gold leaf may stick to the scissors. Use a toothpick to detach. Line the quarter pieces of tissue, gold-side up, on the counter near a freshly wax-paper lined baking sheet.

Melt the remaining chocolate with shortening in a double boiler over hot water. Once melted, remove from heat. Bring out 1 sheet of chilled truffles at a time. Dip each truffle in the melted chocolate, using a candy dipper or a fork and spoon to allow the excess chocolate to fall back into the pot. Gently place each truffle on the baking sheet near the gold leaf. Then carefully take hold of a $1/4$-sheet gold leaf by the tissue and place, gold-side down, onto the freshly dipped truffle and pull away the tissue paper. The gold will stick to the chocolate. Lightly blow on gold leaf if it has not adhered to the truffle. Repeat for the remainder of the truffles. Refrigerate until ready to serve. Makes about 4 dozen truffles.

The Perfect Martini

4 cups gin
1/2 cup dry vermouth
Olives or lemon peel

In a martini pitcher, place plenty of ice, the gin and vermouth. Stir; pour mixture through strainer into chilled martini glasses, adding a lemon peel twist or an olive to each glass. Makes 10 servings.

Custard's

Last Stand

It's easy to see why the desire for the foods that made us feel warm and safe when we were gluttons in utero, embryonic stuffers so to speak, must be kept hidden from that growing army of nouvelle cuisine worshippers who tend to classify a slice of poached chicken breast, accompanied by a green pea or two and a dried beet chip, as a sybaritic repast.

In a world where, as the Duchess of Windsor pointed out, "you can never be too rich or too thin," the poor souls who reach for another roll can become pariahs.

Not since the early Christians met in the catacombs beneath Rome has a group been so persecuted. Some of us even publicly embrace the theory that "less is more," while privately we're hopelessly addicted to such fattening taboos as an heroic slab of meat loaf partnered with a mountain of mashed potatoes awash in rich, brown gravy, or a thick, juicy hamburger smothered in onions and ringed with golden French fries, or white bread slathered with creamy peanut butter, oozing a trail of sticky-sweet grape jelly.

From infancy on, comfort food is either a reward or a bribe. Cry and you get a bottle, finish your carrots and you get dessert. Talk about eating with a loaded deck. It's not too much of a stretch to go from that kind of emotional blackmail to bingeing on blintzes and pigging out on pork chops.

What's wrong with revisiting your childhood for a little solace from a Twinkie or two? When your broker forgets to sell short, or someone suggests a great rinse to cover those new gray hairs or you find yourself on the top of the list for an IRS audit, do you want to curl up with a bowl of oat bran? No sirreeeee. This is a job for tapioca pudding! The British wisely equate the food their nannies served them with their ability to have withstood two world wars, and still ask at the end of dinner, "what's for pudd?"

"Cherry Cobbler is shortcake for the soul."
—*EDNA FERBER*

"Chocolate goes well with sex—before, during, after—it really doesn't matter."
—HELEN GURLEY BROWN

VEAU IS ME

Since the dawn of time, food has been used to comfort the spirit and dull the ache of lone-liness that almost everyone sometimes experiences. People gather to eat and drink at wakes or after funerals. It's often customary to bring something sweet to the bereaved to help soothe the bitterness of loss. These social ceremonies are a source of comfort for the grieving, a reassurance that life will go on.

And how often has the phrase, "food is love," been used to unmask the psyche of the overeater? We repeat it to ourselves to explain our need to reach for a pound of peanut brittle in the midst of a career crisis or when a love affair dies. There's no doubt about it, there are just times when cheesecake equals peace of mind.

Then there's chocolate, that South American aphrodisiac in Swiss clothing. The very first book about this delectable debauchery was written in Spain, in the 1660s, long before Godiva was anything more than a lady with absolutely nothing to wear. The author, however, found the New World delicacy palatable only when two grains of chili were mixed with every 100 grains of cocoa, which only reinforces the observation that some like it hot.

What few realized back then was that cocoa could be made into the most seductive of sweets, sparking not only tooth decay but also the observance of that diabolical holiday, Valentine's Day.

ILLUSTRATION BY CLAUDE SERRE FROM *LA BOUFFE*, 1986, EDITIONS GLÉNAT, GRENOBLE

Only recently has it been discovered that chocolate contains a chemical called phenylethylamine, which produces the same euphoria one feels when one falls in love. It may finally be clear why, of all pleasures, the comfort-food addict most craves chocolate. Not only that, but the sensual sweetie is most enjoyed...*in bed*. The voluptuous quality of chocolate, with it satiny, melt-in-the-mouth enticement, might be the closest thing to making love that a lonelyheart has on a cold winter's night. Now, doesn't that make all those calories worth it?

It would be a great shame to let anyone talk us out of food for comfort. It doesn't matter whether you wind up with a Big Mac or a pound of Beluga caviar, if it makes you feel warm and safe. Is anyone really sure that Freud didn't keep a bag of potato chips handy for that free ten minutes between patients, or that Lincoln didn't have a box of fudge with him on the train to Gettysburg?

In the beginning there was mother's milk, warm and cozy in that miracle of anatomical packaging. From that moment on, food was comfort, food was love, food was power. The proof is in the pudding.

"Sex is good but not as good as fresh, sweet corn."
—GARRISON KEILLOR

"What is patriotism but the love of food one ate as a child?"
—*YIN LUTANG*

Overleaf: *Two Cheeseburgers with Everything (Dual Hamburgers)*, 1962, by Claes Oldenburg

"I like white-trash cooking. Cheeseburgers, the greasier the better. Mashed potatoes served in a scoop, a little dent in the top for the gravy. Drake's Devil Dogs for dessert. Pure pleasure, no known nutrients."
—ORSON BEAN

MIRACLE MEATLOAF
WITH
MUSHROOM GRAVY

FOR MEATLOAF:
1 pound hot Italian sausage meat
2 pounds meatloaf mixture (ground pork, beef and veal)
2 cups chopped onion
1 cup bread crumbs
$^1/2$ cup ketchup
2 eggs, beaten
1 teaspoon Worcestershire sauce
$^1/2$ teaspoon salt
Generous grinding of fresh pepper
4 slices of bacon

FOR MUSHROOM GRAVY:
3 tablespoons butter
2 $^3/4$ cups sliced mushrooms
2 tablespoons flour

2 tablespoons drippings from meatloaf
1 can beef broth
Salt and pepper to taste

Squeeze Italian sausage out of the casings into a large bowl. Add meatloaf mixture, onion, bread crumbs, ketchup, eggs, Worcestershire, salt and pepper. Using clean hands, mix together thoroughly.

In an oval or rectangular pan that will accommodate the meat, shape into a loaf and layer bacon slices diagonally across it. Bake in a preheated 375-degree oven for 1 hour and 45 minutes. Drain fat and reserve for gravy. Turn off the oven. Keep meatloaf warm in the oven while the gravy is prepared.

TO MAKE THE GRAVY: Heat butter in a large saucepan over medium heat. Sauté mushrooms until golden. Add flour and stir. Add hot drippings and stir well. Gradually add broth and stir continually until thickened. When serving, spoon over slices of meatloaf. Makes 8 servings.

Comforting Vanilla Pots à Crème

6 egg yolks
1/2 cup sugar
Pinch of salt
2 cups half-and-half
1/2 cup milk
1 vanilla bean, split
1 teaspoon vanilla extract

Preheat oven to 300 degrees.

Whisk yolks, sugar and salt in bowl until thickened.

Heat half-and-half and milk in saucepan until small bubbles appear around the edges. Scrape seeds from bean into the milk mixture; add bean. Remove from heat and let stand for 5 minutes.

Remove bean from saucepan; strain milk mixture. Pour into yolk mixture, stirring constantly. Stir in vanilla extract. Pour into six 5-ounce ramekins, dividing equally. Gently blot any foam from tops with paper toweling.

Set ramekins in large shallow pan. Pour hot water into pan to depth of 1 inch.

Bake in oven for 1 hour, until custards are set. Remove from pan. Chill. Makes 6 servings.

Chocolate Peanut-Butter Soul Pie

FOR CRUST:
2 1/4 cups chocolate-wafer cookie crumbs
4 tablespoons sugar
6 tablespoons unsalted butter, melted

FOR FILLING:
1 1/4 cups creamy peanut butter
1 (8-ounce) package cream cheese, softened

1 cup sugar
1 3/4 cups chilled heavy cream
2 teaspoons vanilla

FOR TOPPING:
3/4 cup heavy cream
7 ounces semisweet chocolate

Preheat oven to 350 degrees.

TO MAKE THE CRUST: In a medium bowl, combine cookie crumbs and sugar, then add melted butter. Mix well. Press mixture into bottom and up sides of 10-inch pie plate. Bake 10 minutes. Set aside to cool.

TO PREPARE THE FILLING: In a large bowl, cream together peanut butter and cream cheese until smooth. Add sugar and beat well.

In a large, chilled bowl, beat 1 3/4 cups heavy cream and vanilla until soft peaks form. Fold 1/3 into peanut butter mixture. Then gently fold in rest of the whipped cream.

Pile filling into cooled crust. Cover with wax paper and chill at least 5 hours or overnight.

TO MAKE THE TOPPING: Bring 3/4 cup heavy cream to a boil in small saucepan. Remove from heat. Stir in chocolate until smooth. Cool 10 to 15 minutes, until topping begins to thicken. Stir occasionally.

Pour topping over pie and spread evenly. Chill at least 30 minutes, or until topping is set. Makes 10 to 12 servings.

Frances Elizabeth Smith Carter's Three-Layer Devil's Food Cake

FOR CAKE:

2 large eggs

2 cups brown sugar, packed

1 1/2 cups sour cream

2 tablespoons buttermilk or milk

2 1/2 cups sifted flour

1/2 teaspoon baking powder

Pinch of salt

2 teaspoons baking soda

1/2 cup unsweetened cocoa

1/2 cup very hot water

1 1/2 teaspoons pure vanilla extract

FOR BITTERSWEET BUTTERCREAM FROSTING:

6 large egg yolks

1/2 cup sugar

1/2 cup corn syrup

1 pound unsalted butter, softened

8 ounces bittersweet chocolate, melted and slightly cooled

TO MAKE THE CAKE: Grease and flour 3 (8-inch) cake pans. Preheat oven to 350 degrees.

In a large bowl, beat eggs well. Beat in brown sugar. In a separate bowl, mix together the sour cream and buttermilk or milk. Set aside.

Sift together flour, baking powder, salt, baking soda and cocoa.

Add dry ingredients to egg mixture alternately with sour cream mixture and hot water, ending with dry ingredients. Fold in vanilla. Divide batter evenly among pans.

Bake at 350 degrees for about 25 minutes, or until a toothpick inserted in center of cake comes out clean. Let cake layers cool on rack.

━━━━━━

TO MAKE THE FROSTING: In a large bowl, beat the egg yolks until light. Set aside.

Grease a heatproof, glass measuring cup and keep within reach of the stove top. In a small saucepan over medium-high heat, com-bine sugar and corn syrup. Stir constantly until the mixture comes to a rolling boil. Once at a rolling boil, transfer the sugar syrup quickly into the measuring cup.

While beating with a hand-held electric mixer, pour the hot syrup in a steady stream (avoiding the beaters) over the egg yolks. (Use rubber spatula to scrape out syrup from measuring cup.) Beat well.

Beat in the butter and melted chocolate gradually until fully incorporated. Allow buttercream to cool to room temperature before frosting the cake.

Use frosting between the three layers and on sides and top of cake.

━━━━━━

> *"Health food may be good for the conscience but Oreos taste a hell of a lot better."*
> –ROBERT REDFORD

OVERLEAF: ILLUSTRATION BY L. LESLIE BROOKE FROM *THE THREE LITTLE PIGS AND TOM THUMB*, LONDON: 1922, COLLECTION OF FRANCES CONVERSE MASSEY, REPRINTED IN *THE UBIQUITOUS PIG* BY MARILYN NISSENSON & SUSAN JONAS. COURTESY OF *UBIQUITOUS* AUTHORS AND HENRY N. ABRAMS, INC.

FOOD FETISHES

FROM ROME TO NOME

It's certainly fair to say that one man's food fetish is another man's food nightmare. Civilizations throughout the ages have spawned what seem to us bizarre culinary traditions that were to them the height of conventional behavior.

Take, for example, the nomadic Masai of Kenya. Those tall, elegant wanderers, most of whom look like they belong on the cover of *Mirabella*, never found farming an appealing alternative to lion stalking. And when they come home from a hard day of hunting, they kick back with a large glass of cow's blood. Before you grow faint at the thought, is it really so different from consuming a steak, blood-rare, or a primitive plate of steak tartare? Much to their credit, the Masai have even found an efficient method to drain the cow without actually slaughtering it. Count Dracula would have given his eyeteeth for their secret.

Long before the Roman Empire fell with a thud, its most discerning gourmets insisted

Bottle label: Synthetic Blood. Bubble: "Yuk! This is full of colorants."

ILLUSTRATION BY CLAUDE SERRE FROM LA BOUFFE, 1986, EDITIONS GLÉNAT, GRENOBLE

that their favorite dishes be accompanied by the sauce, *liquamen*, which was made of a mixture of fish guts and blood left to grow rancid in the sun until its perfume could be inhaled for miles around.

Actually, the Greeks may have been first to enjoy liquamen. The 5th-century B.C. historian, Herodotus, took the time to note his recipe: Test strength of sea water with an egg. If the egg sinks, water is not salty enough. Put fish (sprats, anchovies or mackerel) in the brine. Boil in earthenware pot. Add oregano. Cool and strain three times.

His sauce seems tamer than the Romans' pungent adaptation, which not only cost a fortune to produce but became the ultimate treat of those rich enough to drink a goblet full. Remains of liquamen were found in jars amid the ruins of Pompeii.

A similar fish sauce is popular in Southeast Asia today.

You Are What You Eat?

People can be defined as much by what they don't eat as by what they do. Anthropologists believe that food taboos are a way for one culture to distinguish itself from another. The worship of the cow by the Hindus means that India is not the place to buy a Burger King franchise. Traditional Jews and Moslems both consider pork a forbidden food and agree that the Three Little Pigs got exactly what they deserved.

Hannibal Lechter Wasn't All Bad

On the other side of the frying pan, most people would put cannibalism at the top of their list of unthinkable food fetishes. Nonetheless, it has been practiced, at one time or another, by almost every ethnic group. You surely remember reading about that tasty little incident at the Donner Pass? The fine art of people-eating is still going on today somewhere in the world.

One form of cannibalism is the mortuary variety. Here, relatives cook the flesh of a beloved deceased, grind up his bones and mix them with a liquid (my preference would be straight gin) which they drink. Even though this appears to be a rather ghoulish example of recycling, it is done as a way of absorbing the dearly departed's best qualities. The Guiaca, a small tribe in South America, are anthropologically famous for their corpse cocktails.

A more straightforward approach to cannibalism is the delight of eating one's vanquished fellow as one of the spoils of war. In a past era, the Maori of New Zealand took almost no food when they went on war parties. Instead, keeping a positive attitude, they were convinced that there would be more than enough to feast on after they conquered their adversaries. In fact, they believed that the best way to prepare for the battle was by discussing how sweet their enemies would surely taste. Anthropologists point out that the diners believed they would gain the strength of their foes by eating them.

Papua New Guinea was, and in a few pockets may still be, a testing ground for the theories of cannibalism. One Papuan tribe had its own spin on food as a weapon. The group believed that gluttony brought with it ruination and madness. This is not far removed from the fears that are expressed daily in the fitting rooms at Saks or Barney's. But for these Papuans, food had

Some Papua New Guinea tribes practiced ritual cannibalism. Others won battles by refusing all food. Is this mountain man what he ate, or what he didn't?

the power to destroy enemies, since overeating was thought both irresistible and shameful. And so an enemy's doorstep was covered with pigs, yams and the most tempting of fruits and nuts. It was hoped that unable to resist, the opponent would eat all day and then surrender, too mortified to show his face in the village.

It's a story heard at Weight Watchers meetings all over the world.

Another food-chain startler is dining on what others regard as house pets. In Korea, dog is as routinely served as cat is in some of Africa. In the mountains of Ecuador, the Zumbagua believe that serving a roasted guinea pig is a sign that a friendship or a love affair will be cemented.

"I believe that if I ever had to practice cannibalism I might manage it if there were enough tarragon around."
–JAMES BEARD

A Chip Off the Old Block

The oddest vegetarian tale is that of a man from Chicago who consumed a birch tree that measured over eleven feet in height. It took him eighty-nine hours to chew up the branches, leaves, and trunk—a case, perhaps, of a bark worse than a bite. The man survived his woody repast and pocketed the handsome $10,000 prize that had been offered by a Chicago radio station. Where is Joyce Kilmer when you need him?

Also in the strong-teeth department is the Eskimo habit of chewing on the bones of fish or bear until they become a paste that can be swallowed. After that, chewing on seal blubber seems Epicurean.

Simply No Accounting for Tastes

Insect gourmands are dedicated to scratching their culinary itches. Some Mexicans prefer their locusts deep-fried in oil, lightly misted with Tabasco and then sprinkled with oregano.

If that doesn't make your taste buds tingle, then perhaps Madagascar cockroaches, over two inches long, marinated in wine vinegar before being served as hors d'oeuvres, will. Yet another unsettling tidbit in Madagascar, just in case you're contemplating a vacation there, is mealworm larvae stuffed into a flaky *samosa* and sautéed to a golden brown.

Women who work in Chinese silk factories enjoy a perk livelier than the tea break. While weaving the silk on their looms, they wait for the silkworm chrysalis to drop from the cocoon. The weavers pop chrysalides into their mouths like jellybeans.

In China, ants and the liquid made from their formic acid are routinely eaten to relieve the pain of arthritis and ease the symptoms of asthma and hepatitis. In the province of Harbin, Queen Ant wine is as highly prized as fine cognac and has almost the same kick. A nectar of crushed ants, distilled to a potent 80 proof, is said to make hair lustrous and benefit both the pancreas and spleen. In China, ants seem to be the answer for almost everything.

"Favorite animal: steak!"
—Fran Liebowitz

"Statistics show that of those who contract the habit of eating, very few survive."
— Wallace Irwin

Oogruk Flippers

1 oogruk
blubber

'Cut the flippers off a small oogruk. Put flippers in fresh blubber [on ice] and let them stay there for 2 weeks. Take the loose fur off the flipper. Cut flipper into small pieces and eat the meat."
—Eskimo Cookbook, *prepared by students of Shishmaref Day School, Shishmaref, Alaska, 1952*

Chocolate Ants

1,742 large ants (if they are small, use 2,044)
3 cups melted chocolate
1 teaspoon sugar

'Catch ants at a picnic site and keep them in a glass jar to which you have added the sugar to keep them happy. (Unhappy ants are liable to go sour before processing.) At home, pick up each ant with tweezers and remove entrails with a small, very sharp knife-edge. This will take about 400 hours. If you are in a hurry, eliminate this step; you will never know the difference. Dip each ant into melted chocolate and place on wax paper. If any of them are still able to crawl off the paper, let them go—be a good sport!" Serves six at your own risk.

—*SEARCHABLE ONLINE ARCHIVE OF RECIPES (http://soar.Berkeley.EDU/recipes)*

The Dinner Party, 1991, by Janet Seaward

Sizzling Simple Sausage

1 pound ground pork
1 teaspoon salt
1 teaspoon ground sage, or to taste
1/4 teaspoon cayenne pepper
1 egg

In a large bowl, using clean hands, work all ingredients together thoroughly.

Form into 4 large patties or 6 smaller ones. Place in a heavy skillet and brown on both sides over fairly high heat. Then turn heat down, add 1/4 cup water and cook 10 to 15 minutes more, covered. Makes 4 to 6 servings.

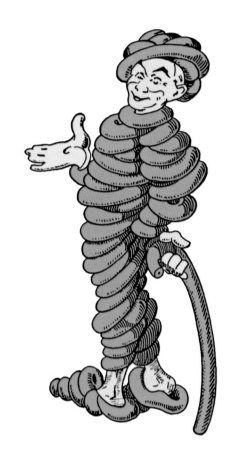

"Men are like sausages. Whatever you stuff them with, that they will bear with them."
—*Alexei Tolstoy*

A QUICHE

IN THE DARK

The role of the gourmet in French society was greatly enhanced by the birth of the French restaurant. The true restaurant was a result of a little dustup known as the French Revolution. Before the Revolution, only the nobility was able to appreciate the joys of gastronomy.

There had long been roadside taverns and inns where people could go for drink and travelers might eat, but those were seedy, unwholesome and often dangerous. People rarely ventured far from home to enjoy the pleasures of the commercial table. The Revolution changed all that. The cooks who had worked in the kitchens of the aristocracy were all dressed up with nowhere to go. It finally occurred to them to find places where they could be at home on their own ranges. Voilà—a cozy place to buy your onion soup, bowl by bowl.

The large, central table was called the host's table or *la table d'hôte*. The humble owner-cook became less and less humble as Saturday Night Restaurant Fever spread. Now the bourgeoisie could tuck into food that was once enjoyed by silver-spooners.

One From Column A or Column B or Column C

The first restaurant-goer to send his Veal Prince Orloff back to the kitchen because the sauce was not "silky" enough, had bestowed upon him, by his awed tablemates, the designation, gourmet. After all, someone had to tell the rest of us what we were eating and whether it was, in fact, edible.

The gourmet's evil twin is the gourmand, who is marginally interested in the quality of the food he eats; but his engine is really fueled by quantity. The best way to tell the twins apart is to watch as they go about the ritual of dinner.

The gourmet, believing that you truly are what you eat, eats only the finest, and he does it with great deliberation. Each mouthful is held on the tongue to be fully savored and, of course, evaluated. The gourmet, if not preparing his or her own meal, makes sure that it is created by the finest chef to be found, and presented in the finest temple of gastronomy that he or she can afford.

The gourmand will sometimes venture into the same rarefied territory but when the menu is presented, he wants to talk turkey. No soul-searching for the perfect fish course to offset the heartiness of the boeuf Bourguignonne, no pondering the benefit of an aged Brie to accompany a salad of field greens—no, not on your puttanesca. After a brief glance, he knows just what will satisfy his formidable hunger, and can rattle off choices without a moment's hesitation, except to ask what additions can be ordered. The gourmand makes sure that the only sliver of tablecloth left bare is the spot where his elbow will rest. Then, let the eating begin!

Gourmets may be dedicated to the pleasures of superb dining and gourmands to the pleasures of the full belly, but true gluttons are much more difficult to recognize. They often do most of their eating alone, in secret.

"To be a gourmet you must start early, as you begin riding early to be a good horseman.
You must live in France; your father must have been a gourmet.
Nothing in your life must interest you but your stomach.
With hands trembling, you must approach the meal about which you have
worried all day, and risk dying of a stroke if it isn't perfect."
—Ludwig Bemelmans

:THIS LITTLE PIG:
WENT TO MARKET

FACING PAGE: ILLUSTRATION BY WALTER CRANE FROM *THIS LITTLE PIG WENT TO MARKET*, LONDON: 1895. FRANCES CONVERSE MASSEY COLLECTION. REPRINTED IN *THE UBIQUITOUS PIG* BY MARILYN NISSENSON & SUSAN JONAS. COURTESY OF *UBIQUITOUS* AUTHORS AND HENRY N. ABRAMS, INC.

CREAM AND PUNISHMENT

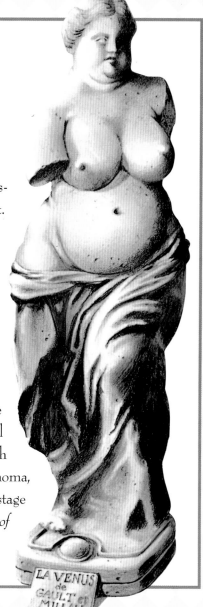

The most pathetic of all specimens is the fallen gourmet. While on the outside he's a paragon of selectivity and discernment, underneath there is a gourmand screaming to get out. The manifestations of this syndrome are somewhat difficult to identify. At first, it's just a question of another wedge of Stilton because of its "unusual veining." But from there it can escalate into a rare case of "gourmet bulimia," which is a devilish pattern of haute cuisine/purge/haute cuisine/purge. Finally, the insatiable gourmet is making reservations at food festivals around the country.

The helpless gourmet visits the Frog-Eating Contest in Rayne, Louisiana to observe the judging, or sits on the dais at the Virginia Flapjack Festival in Great Falls. One day, unable to control his obscene urges, he transforms into a contestant. When faced with the most private parts of a calf, at the Testicle Festival in Vinita, Oklahoma, he uses the excuse that "prairie oysters" are a great delicacy. The last stage of his hellish existence is attending contests for the *Guinness Book of World Records* to ogle the world's largest pizza or the heaviest

ILLUSTRATION BY CLAUDE SERRE FROM LA BOUFFE, 1986, EDITIONS GLÉNAT, GRENOBLE

zucchini. He loses all sense of reality when he's invited to participate in the making of the world's biggest banana split (7,005 feet long with 11,400 bananas, topped with 1,500 gallons of ice cream). Will there ever be an end to his torture?

Unfortunately, the danger exists that he will one day receive an engraved note from Le Cirque, the altar at which every gourmet worth his hollandaise worships, informing him that his reservations have been canceled for the rest of the year and his name removed from the permanent guest book. Some things you just can't keep a secret.

A t a Potato Festival in Mantua, Ohio, one vat of mashed potatoes weighed in at 10, 236 pounds.

Circe, 1927, by George Grosz

GIFT OF MR. AND MRS. WATER BAREISS AND AN ANONYMOUS DONOR. PHOTO © THE MUSEUM OF MODERN ART, NEW YORK

Gluttony Today

What once passed for the sin of gluttony is now psychologically part of the national psyche called an eating disorder. Those who think themselves sophisticated and dietetically savvy subscribe to the theory that what matters is not what the tubbies are eating but what's eating them. While our old friend, Thomas Aquinas, identified gluttony as a breach of religious devotion, a more enlightened and sympathetic society knows that it can be a real threat to longevity.

"Nouvelle cuisine, roughly translated, means: "I can't believe I spent $96 and I'm still hungry."
—*MIKE KALINA*

Bounty, 1996, by Nancy Hagin

Real-Man Quiche

This four-cheese leek quiche makes a fabulous appetizer. Or, accompanied by a green salad, it's a great lunch dish for real people.

Single 9-inch unbaked piecrust
2 leeks
1 tablespoon butter
1 1/4 teaspoons chopped fresh marjoram
1 1/2 teaspoons chopped fresh thyme
2 ounces goat cheese

3/4 cup half-and-half
3 eggs, beaten
1/2 cup grated Gruyere
1/2 cup grated Parmesan
1/4 cup grated soft Fontina

Preheat oven to 375 degrees. Bake pie shell for 5 to 10 minutes. Do not let crust brown. Set aside.

Clean leeks thoroughly and slice crosswise very thinly. In a medium sauté pan, heat butter over medium-high heat and sauté leeks until caramelized. Add chopped herbs and stir to distribute evenly. Turn off heat and set aside.

In a large bowl, mash goat cheese with a little of the half-and-half. Add beaten eggs and then the rest of the half-and-half. Stir in the grated cheeses and then add the leek-herb mixture. Pour into prepared piecrust. Bake for 30 minutes until the top is lightly browned.

Eight servings or more as hors d'oeuvres.

Glorious Garlic Mashed Potatoes

8 to 10 cloves garlic
1/4 cup olive oil
2 1/2 pounds Yukon Gold potatoes
1/2 cup heavy cream, warmed
1 stick butter, softened
Salt and pepper to taste

Peel garlic cloves and roughly mash with the side of a large knife. In a small sauté pan, heat the oil over medium heat and sauté the mashed garlic until golden. Set aside.

Wash and peel potatoes. Cut into 2-inch cubes and place in a pot large enough to hold them. Cover with water and bring to boil. Boil until potatoes are fork-tender. Remove from heat, drain, and return to the pot.

Add heavy cream, butter, garlic and olive oil to the potatoes and mash with a potato masher until they reach the desired consistency. (For very smooth potatoes, use an electric mixer to beat the ingredients together.)

Add salt and pepper to taste. Mix well. Serve piping hot. Makes 8 to 10 servings.

BAKED FOIE GRAS À LA VARENNE

Published instructions for *foie gras cuit dans les cendres* come from the comprehensive 17th-century French cookbook written by Francois-Pierre de La Varenne, chef of the Marquis D'Uxelles. La Varenne's work was so popular with both the aristocracy and bourgeoisie that between 1651 and 1721 it enjoyed 30 printings. La Varenne naturally ordered this delicacy cooked in the hot cinders of a fireplace. That would still work, but we've allowed for the possibility that you might find it handier to bake the foie gras in your oven.

1 fresh foie gras* (approximately 1 3/4 pounds)
4 or 5 sheets wax paper
Pure pork lard
1 clove
1/4 of a bay leaf
2 or 3 sprigs fresh thyme
5 to 6 peppercorns
1 teaspoon salt
1 pound very thinly sliced fatback

Remove any parts of the liver that may have been stained green by the gallbladder as well as any fibers or skin.

Generously grease wax paper on both sides with lard.

Pound in a mortar (or grind in an electric mill): clove, bay leaf, thyme, peppercorns and salt. Reduce to a fine powder. Sprinkle half this mixture over goose liver. Wrap liver in fatback strips. Sprinkle remaining herb mixture over it. Wrap liver in sheets of wax paper. In order to keep the juices from leaking out, alternate the directions of the paper, wrapping first sheet lengthwise, second crosswise, and so on.

Bury the package in very hot cinders of a fireplace, or bake in a hot oven (425 degrees) for one hour.

Let cool. Unwrap, remove fatback and serve with small, thin toast. Makes 8 appetizer servings.

———

*Fresh foie gras is available from, and can be shipped most places by, Urbani, Long Island City, NY: 718-392-5050, and D'Artagnan: 1-800-DARTAGN or www. dartagnan.com.

———

CHAPTER EIGHT

CINEMA

GASTRONOMIQUE

If one picture is worth a thousand words, then a film featuring food is worth a million culinary fantasies. The delight of watching people indulge themselves as we sit in the dark and munch on our popcorn is something that the big cheeses in Hollywood have become very much aware of. They know that romance, action-adventure and musicals aren't the only things that lure the public into their shiny new multiplexes.

There have been films that used food for comedy as far back as Mack Sennett's Keystone Kops with their custard pie obsession. Later, in *Public Enemy* (1931), Jimmy Cagney applied a grapefruit to the face of poor Mae Clarke. It was Jimmy's rather violent way of making sure that she had her allotted amount of vitamin C for the day, and probably the first time that a citrus fruit was used as a weapon.

The 1971 screen adaptation of Roald Dahl's *Willie Wonka and the Chocolate Factory* is a toothsome fantasy for chocoholics of any age—better than a trip to Hershey, Pennsylvania.

As audiences became more sophisticated in their eating habits, so did food images on film. One of the better-known examples of the food-film genre (which, by some odd coincidence, just happens to have been taken from a novel by your humble author and her husband) is *Who is Killing the Great Chefs of Europe?* (1978). Its central theme is preoccupation with food, both in the world of haute cuisine and the not-so-haute-cuisine world of fast-food factories. Robert Morley brought his not inconsiderable talents to the role of the publisher who finds he can only diet by murdering the world-famous chefs whom he blames for all his problems.

Great Chefs was followed by many other films, some of them foreign made, that use food as a metaphor for lust, greed, sex, and last, but not least, the star of our story, gluttony. One of the more erotic of the bunch is the award-winning *Like Water for Chocolate* (Mexico 1991), in which the family cook, hopelessly in love with a man whom she can never marry, shows her devotion by creating extravagant dishes to seduce him. It's her delectable way of making love.

Another erotic food fight, one that ends with more spilled than milk, is *The Cook, the Thief, His Wife and Her Lover* (England and France, 1989). At La Hollandaise Restaurant, there is nonstop gluttony from dusk till dawn, and the menu features murder, sex, revenge and a pretty decent rack of lamb. Of all the silver screen's valentines to the food aficionado, none is as heartwarming and hilarious as *Big Night* (United States, 1997), which is about two bumbling brothers who open a restaurant on a dream and not much more.

MORE FOOD FLICKS

LA GRAND BOUFFE: This could almost be called a porno flick about food and depravity. Its orgiastic detail both shocks and rivets. The main characters lock themselves away to eat without restraint, to death, one might say. It takes a strong stomach to view this one.

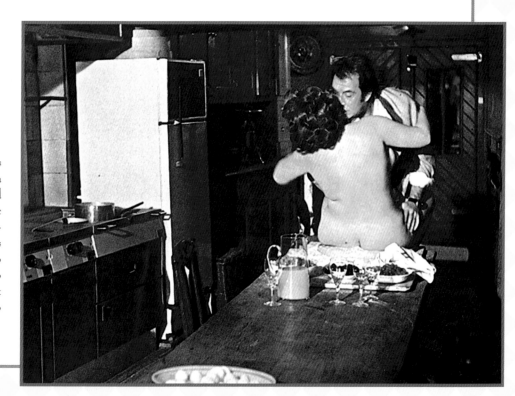

BABETTE'S FEAST: In this extraordinary film, based on an Isak Dinesen story, a passionate French cook wins the lottery. After years of having lived among people to whom food represents only basic nourishment, she creates a superb meal which awakens them to the artistry of her soul. (Panorama/Nordisk/Danish Film Institute, 1987)

Facing page: *LITTLE SHOP OF HORRORS:* The first film of this bizarre story was directed by Roger Corman in 1960; the Technicolor remake, which appeared in 1986, incorporates tunes from a play based on the Corman movie. In all versions, the leafy tale stars a delightfully carnivorous plant named Audrey.

TOM JONES: This wonderfully bawdy movie (based on the Henry Fielding 19th-century novel) of the adventures of irrepressible, captivating Tom, sports great eating scenes. In the pièce de no résistance, Tom (played by Albert Finney) sits across the table from his conquest-to-be, lasciviously savoring a ripe pear between tongue and teeth. During other Tony Richardson-directed bites, both beef and poultry are more kinetically devoured than they have been before or since in movieland. (Woodfall/United Artists-Lopert, 1963)

Hollywood stars lead bits of their lives as we do. Heather Locklear likes to swing by Taco Bell more often than she would have it known. Liv Tyler and Ashley Judd are French fry fanatics. Jennifer Love Hewett prefers classic Coke to Lala Land's mineral water. Matt Damon's X-rated snack is chocolate cake, while Winona Ryder eats enough Eskimo Pies to rate her own igloo.

HISTORY OF THE WORLD, PART I: In Mel Brooks' glorious satire of ancient Rome, Dom Deluise does a hilarious take on Emperor Nero. Will the real pig please stand up? (Brooksfilms, 1961)

Roast Suckling Pig

1 (approximately 18-lb.) suckling pig
2 tablespoons olive oil
6 garlic cloves, smashed
2 tablespoons chopped fresh rosemary

2 tablespoons salt
2 teaspoons freshly ground pepper
2 quarts ginger ale
1 large red apple (optional)

Preheat oven to 450 degrees.

Rub olive oil all over the pig. Slip underneath the skin garlic, rosemary, salt and pepper. Rub some of the herb mixture inside the cavity, too. If you are going to serve the pig with an apple in its mouth, use a large wad of foil to hold the pig's mouth open during roasting.

Place pig on a rack in a roasting pan and cover loosely with foil. Roast for 1 1/2 hours, then uncover the pig. Pour about 2 cups of ginger ale over the pig and continue roasting for about another hour. Baste whenever the liquid begins to dry up, and again during the last 15 minutes of roasting. (All the

ginger ale may not be necessary.) If the pig appears to be browning too quickly, turn heat down to 425 degrees.

The pig is done when it is well-browned and a leg wiggles easily at the joint or when a meat thermometer, inserted in its thigh away from a bone, registers 160 degrees.

If presenting the pig with apple in mouth, remove foil from its mouth and insert apple. Makes 10-12 servings of pork.

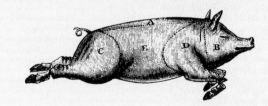

Tom Jones Fried Chicken

This fried chicken is juicy and crisp, but not loaded with breading.

1 chicken, cut into 8 pieces
1 quart buttermilk
Tabasco or fresh lemon juice
1 cup all-purpose flour, approximately

2 teaspoons salt
1 1/2 teaspoons freshly ground black pepper
1 pound pure lard

Place chicken in a stainless-steel, glass, enamel or ceramic dish and cover with buttermilk. (You may not need all the buttermilk.) Add several drops of Tabasco or juice of 1 lemon. Cover. Let chicken marinate in refrigerator for at least 1 hour, or as long as 8.

Remove chicken and use paper towels to pat off excess buttermilk.

Using a fork, combine flour, salt and pepper in a shallow dish or pie plate. Dredge each piece of chicken in flour, coating thoroughly.

Melt lard in a cast-iron skillet (you may not need the whole pound but the melted lard should be about an inch deep in the skillet); heat until almost smoking. Do not crowd the skillet when you place chicken pieces in it. Brown the chicken pieces at high heat. Watch chicken carefully and adjust heat to keep skin from burning. Turn and brown the other side of each portion. Remove pieces as they are browned.

Return all chicken to the pan; if all the pieces will not fit in your skillet, layer them in so dark meat is on the bottom and white meat is on the top. Partially cover skillet. Cook 15-20 minutes until chicken is done, but still juicy. Makes 4 servings.

CHAPTER NINE

TOQUES OFF

TO DREAMERS

The journey from gluttony to gastronomy has been long and full of twists. It started with Thomas Aquinas, who thought that an extra slice of honey cake was enough to send you straight to hell. Centuries later, a philosopher and all-around bon vivant named Anthelme Brillat-Savarin made history by believing that not eating the most extraordinary slice of honey cake that could be made was a betrayal of one's God-given palate. It's a good thing these two never crossed forks.

Anyone who has ever looked to the culinary heights for the brightest Michelin superstars in the firmament has Brillat-Savarin to blame. Like the hero of *Jacques and the Beanstalk*, he planted the seeds from which sprouted the philosophy of the art of fine cuisine. His delightfully witty and worldly compendium on the art of eating, *The Physiology of Taste*, published in 1826, made him a legend. A culinary line was drawn in the sauce *velouté*. Brillat-Savarin's work was revered as the holy grail of gastronomy.

Brillat-Savarin was creating his work on the pleasures of the table while the great Antonin Carême, known as the "king of chefs and the chef of kings" was putting pleasures right on the table. After leaving the kitchen of diplomat Charles Talleyrand, Carême furthered his delicious reputation by working for the Prince Regent of England (the future George IV) and then Alexander I of Russia. It was in the czar's service that Carême invented—hold on to your toques—Russian dressing.

Some say that the tall white hat worn by chefs was designed to allow air circulation around the head of a cook toiling in stifling kitchen heat. Another theory holds that the toque's shape derives from the hats worn by Greek Orthodox priests. The color, white, distinguished the cooks from others who inhabited the monasteries. Which story is true? Take your choice.

The sayings of Brillat-Savarin: "Tell me what you eat and I will tell you what you are."

FACING PAGE: MENU COLLECTION, NEW YORK ACADEMY OF MEDICINE

LES APHORISMES DE BRILLAT-SAVARIN

« dis-moi ce que tu manges, je te dirai ce que tu es »

Carême dessert towers

Beyond his exquisite sauces and souf-
flés, Carême was master of the spun-sugar
architectural design. His creations rose to
heights of three or four feet above the table
and were covered with intricate designs and
embellishments, which he cast from molds
he'd also designed. His dessert tables were lavish, artistic expressions of his culinary genius.

Carême was the most famous and richest chef of his day—talk about making the dough
rise. He went on to write cookbooks, most of which are still used today, and to open a cooking
school that produced a whole generation of disciples who carried their master's work all over the
world. The golden age of the French chef began with Antonin Carême.

The Suite Life

Just over a century ago, two bold dreamers joined forces to open the Hotel Savoy in London.
One of them was Caesar Ritz and the other was a soon-to-be internationally famous chef
named Auguste Escoffier.

Escoffier, who had enjoyed an illustrious career in Paris and in dazzling kitchens on the
Riviera, shared with Ritz the dream of a hotel that would attract the *crème de la crème* of British

Bistro is the word Russian soldiers, stationed in Paris at the turn of the last century, left behind. "Bistro, bistro," the Russkies shouted, hoping for faster service in the cafes. In Russian, "bistro" means "quick." The bistro became known as a place you could get a bowl of onion soup in a hurry.

society. The fly in the ragout was that the English still considered hotels to be one step up from brotheldom. This fabulous dream team agreed that making the dining room a great success would entice people to stay the night. Because of the brilliance of Escoffier's kitchen, the Savoy quickly became a mecca for the most glamorous names of the day. Escoffier had realized that to attract business, there is nothing like a dame. He created the thinnest of toast for the renowned singer, Dame Nellie Melba, to nibble between arias. He went on to whip up *pêche Melba* when the very same lady was unable to decide between peaches and ice cream for her dessert. So much for the diets of divas.

The whisk of greatness had passed from Carême to Escoffier, who went on with Ritz to create a grand hotel on the Place Vendome. To this day, the dining room of the Ritz in Paris serves Escoffier-inspired dishes.

FROM THE SUBLIME TO THE RIDICULOUS

LET'S HEAR IT FOR:

☛ Quadequina, who served popcorn to the Plymouth Pilgrims at that first Thanksgiving in 1621.

☛ The 1889 inventor of a chewing-gum locket, fitted with an anti-corrosive lining. Despite its seeming practicality, this gizmo never replaced the bedpost as the preferred overnight resting place for a wad of gum.

☛ Frank Perdue, whose dream came home to roost when, after putting a chicken in every pot, he starred in his own commercials to make sure we were listening to him.

☛ The unknown Chinese woman or man who, two million years ago, mixed rice, milk and snow together to come up with ice cream.

☛ Marco Polo who recreated the chilly taste sensation when he returned to Italy in 1295.

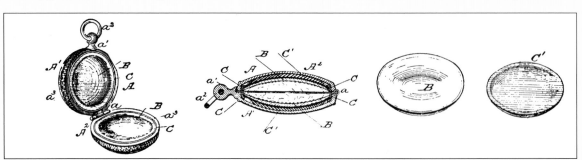

Chewing Gum Locket

☛ Italo Marcioni who had the wit, in 1903, to stuff ice cream into a folded waffle, thereby creating ice cream in a cone—which caused a near riot at the World's Fair in St. Louis.

☛ U.S. Patent-holder #895,515 who perfected a tapeworm trap in 1854. Before using it, the tapeworm sufferer was required to fast for several hours. The small trap, attached to a string, was then baited with a morsel of food. The patient swallowed it, leaving a bit of string dangling from his mouth. The patient could then swallow nothing else to ensure that the parasite became ravenous enough to take the bait. Some time before the patient starved to death, presumably, the worm would slither toward the food, whereupon the trap would snap close on its head. It was then incumbent upon the host to draw up the string very slowly, lest the worm's six-foot-long body be severed from its top before removal. This contraption promised to spare the sufferer the risk of medicine. Why was it not a market success? My guess is the worm turned.

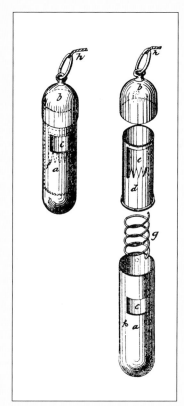

Tapeworm Trap.

☛ Ray Crock, who believed in building a faster, better, burger, and wound up with a billion dollar bun-anza under golden arches.

"A woman should never be seen eating or drinking, unless it's lobster salad and Champagne."
—LORD BYRON

Chefs now make *Forbes'* annual list of the most powerful, highest-paid American moguls. The top five pâté pushers are Wolfgang Puck (who earned $10.5 million in 1998), Jean-Georges Vongerichten, Daniel Boulud, Nobu Matsuhisa and Emeril Lagasse.

We've all been guilty of eating too much at one time or another, whether alone in a room with our discarded candy wrappers or out at a pancake-eating contest. That doesn't make us sinners. It makes us guilty of wanting to enjoy life to its fullest. Food can be as much of a celebration of life as a fine play, a party or a new love affair. Food is often more satisfying. When the chips are down, a bag of Ruffles might just make the difference between despair and renewal. The truth is the fine art of eating is the art no one has been able to live without.

"One cannot think well, love well, sleep well, if one has not dined well."
—*VIRGINIA WOOLF*

An Oregon woman who ordered hamburgers at a drive-through McDonald's was given chicken nuggets, instead. Enraged, she crawled through the window, bombarded the employees with her unwanted food and destroyed the cash register. Could it be that she wanted it her way?

Escoffier's Lobster Newburg

Auguste Escoffier asserted that preparing *homard à la Newburg* with boiled lobster was "more correct" than using raw lobster.

DOREL, 1920

3 (1 1/2 pound) lobsters
3 carrots, cut into 2-inch chunks
2 ribs celery, cut into 2-inch chunks
1 onion halved and stuck with 2 cloves
7 whole peppercorns
A few sprigs of fresh thyme
Several sprigs of fresh parsley
1/4 cup salt
1/4 cup lemon juice
1 package individual puff pastry shells
2 tablespoons unsalted butter
1/4 cup Madeira
1 cup heavy cream
1/2 cup lobster broth
Salt and pepper
1 egg yolk

In a lobster pot or large stockpot, place carrots, celery, onion, peppercorns, thyme, parsley, salt and lemon juice. Add 2 1/2 gallons of water. Bring to a boil. When liquid has reached a rolling boil, parboil lobsters for 4 1/2 minutes. Remove lobsters promptly with tongs and let cool until just warm to the touch.

Let broth simmer as you shell the lobster.

Remove the meat and roe (if there is any) over a bowl to collect lobster juice. Reserve juice and shells. Cut tail and claw meat into 1/2-inch slices. Place meat in a bowl and chill until ready to use.

Add lobster shells to the broth. Keep broth on a low boil for 1 1/2 hours. Then strain broth through a sieve, and discard the solids. Reserve 1/2 cup of the broth and freeze the rest for later use.

Bake the puff pastry shells now, according to package instructions, and keep warm in the oven.

Take the lobster out of the refrigerator. In a large sauté pan, over medium heat melt butter until bubbly. Sauté lobster meat for 1 or 2 minutes and season with salt and pepper.

Turn lobster pieces once or twice. Remove the lobster from the pan to a plate. Cover the plate so lobster meat stays warm.

Keep the sauté pan on the heat and add Madeira. Stir to deglaze pan. Raise heat to high and then add the heavy cream and lobster broth. Bring to a boil and reduce until the sauce covers the back of a spoon. Turn the heat to low.

In a small bowl, add 2 spoonfuls of lobster sauce to the egg yolk and beat together.

Add the lobster meat, any roe, and juices to the sauté pan and then stir in the egg yolk mixture. Stir until the sauce thickens a bit. Taste and adjust seasoning.

Spoon lobster and sauce into individual pastry shells. Makes 4 servings.

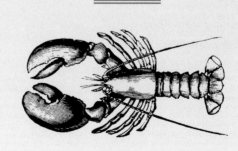

Wicked Waffles and Ice Cream

Warm homemade waffles served with Lorene Smith's double-vanilla ice cream are bliss. Mrs. Smith was a Missouri country cook, and we thought that eating her hand-cranked ice cream brought us as close to heaven as we'd ever come. But if you don't have time to approach paradise quite yet, this double-vanilla custard can be frozen in an electric ice-cream maker and still taste very, very good.

═══════════

FOR THE ICE CREAM:
4 egg yolks
1 1/2 cups granulated sugar
1/4 cup brown sugar
1 teaspoon salt
1/2 cup flour
1 quart milk
1 vanilla bean, split
2 teaspoons pure vanilla extract
3 cups heavy cream

FOR THE WAFFLES:
3 1/2 cups all-purpose flour
2 tablespoons sugar
2 1/2 teaspoons baking soda
1 teaspoon salt
3 eggs, separated
3 cups buttermilk
1/2 cup butter, melted

═══════════

TO MAKE THE ICE CREAM: In a heavy-bottomed saucepan, make a paste of the egg yolks, white and brown sugars, salt, flour and a little of the milk. Gradually stir in the remaining milk, making sure that no lumps form. Add vanilla bean. Cook, stirring, over medium heat until custard mixture thickens. Stir constantly, or almost constantly, so the custard does not scorch.

Remove custard from fire and add vanilla extract. Cover surface of custard with waxed paper to keep a skin from forming, and refrigerate until well-chilled. When the custard is completely cold, remove vanilla bean. (If you are not sure the custard is lumpless, you may also strain it at this point.)

Pour the cold custard into canister of a 1-gallon ice-cream freezer. Add heavy cream, filling to no more than 4 inches from the top of the freezer. (The mixture will expand as it freezes to become ice cream.) Freeze, according to machine manufacturer's directions. Makes 1 gallon of ice cream.

TO PREPARE WAFFLES: Combine flour, sugar, baking soda and salt in a bowl. Beat egg yolks in a large bowl; stir in buttermilk. Add flour mixture to buttermilk mixture and mix just enough to blend. Stir in butter.

Beat egg whites in a large bowl until stiff but do not let dry peaks form. Gently fold whites into batter just to blend.

Make 8 waffles in a waffle iron. Stack between sheets of waxed paper on a large baking sheet; keep warm in 225-degree oven. When ready to serve, top each waffle with 2 or more scoops of double-vanilla ice cream.

Early 20th-century menus for Escoffier soireés celebrate
cuisines from around the world.

"God forgives the sin of gluttony."
—*CATALAN PROVERB*

RAYMOND LOEFFLER

Sylvia Carter (left) and E. Clarke Reilly edited and tested the recipes in this book.

Sylvia Carter is *Newsday's* food columnist and the author of *Eats: The Guide to The Best Little Restaurants in New York.*

E. Clarke Reilly, who has cooked and catered professionally in New York and Boston, is a *Newsday* assistant editor.

Bernadette Wheeler, a *Newsday* food writer, also contributed to *Gluttony's* Carte Blanche recipes.

SIN SERIES

VOLUME II

Have you read?

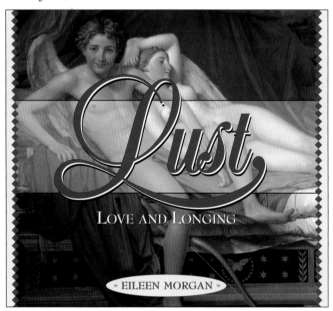

Lust

LOVE AND LONGING

EILEEN MORGAN

www.redrockpress.com